Challenge
TO CHANGE

LORD, What Do You Want Me to Do?

DION S. TAN

CHALLENGE TO CHANGE

Copyright © 2024 Dion S. Tan
First edition published 2024.

The moral right of the author to full ownership of the copyright of *Challenge to Change* has been asserted. All rights are reserved. The book may not be reproduced in part or whole without prior written permission from the author, Dion S. Tan.

Cover Design, Interior Formatting and proofreading by:

WordWyze Publishing Ltd
http://wordwyze.nz

Published by Cast Your Net Publishing

Copies of *Challenge to Change* are available in New Zealand to be purchased direct from Cast Your Net Publishing at castyournetpublishing@gmail.com

Unless otherwise specified, all Scripture quotations are taken from New King James Version (NKJV) copyright© 1982 by Thomas Nelson. Used by permission. Www.thomasnelson.com.

Scripture quotations marked (CEV) are taken from Contemporary English Version® Copyright © 1995 American Bible Society. All rights reserved.

Scripture quotations marked (CSB) are taken from Christian Standard Bible (CSB), copyright © 2017, by Holman Bible Publishers, Used by permission www.CSBible.com.

Scripture quotations marked (NIVUK) are taken from Holy Bible, New International Version® Anglicized, NIV® Copyright © 1979, 1984, 2011 by Biblica, Inc.® Used by permission. All rights reserved worldwide.

Printed in New Zealand by YourBooks.

A catalogue record for this book is available
from the National Library of New Zealand.

Paperback ISBN:	978-0-473-72789-5
Epub ISBN:	978-0-473-72790-1

Challenge
TO CHANGE

LORD, What Do You Want Me to Do?

DION S. TAN

Contents

DEDICATION V

ACKNOWLEDGEMENTS VII

INTRODUCTION 9

CATALYST OF CHANGE 15

PROFESSIONAL PARALYSIS 43

CHOSEN AND CONSECRATED 63

VOCATIONAL EPIPHANY 79

ITINERARY OF AN IMMIGRANT 97

DRIVEN BY A PROMISE 111

FOREKNOWLEDGE 135

THE ANSWER TO MY JOURNEY 147

ABOUT THE AUTHOR 150

Dedication

To my family, who collectively joined me in my journey with this book, their prayers, love and support; my children: Dan, Cera, Braeden and my sister Peggie.

And to my loving wife, Debbie, who saw each step of the way and witnessed God's miracles.

Acknowledgements

I want to thank the people who walked with me on this journey:
Pam Driver, who read through my raw writing.
Joelle Theresa Tantuco, who used
'Asian reading glasses' through this manuscript.
Graham Pedersen, whose Kiwi editing eye brings fresh vision.
Joyce Go, whose writings, personality and prayers
have given great wisdom in writing.
Danny Niñal, your wisdom and creativity as a writer define you.
Colleen Kaluza, your professional services inspired new ideas
Thank you for all your help and support for this book.
And NZ Christian Writers for the fellowship and vision.

*To everything,
There is a season,
A time for every purpose under heaven:
Ecclesiastes 3:1*

Introduction

Change Perspective

I NOTICED SOMETHING WAS DIFFERENT when I walked out one day for my usual hour's walk around my neighbourhood. The air is getting a little nippy, and when I walk along the reserve's footpath, the trees that have faithfully greeted me each morning, waving their leaves and branches, are now turning yellow. They fill the road with their leaves. Autumn is here. And I know the season is changing.

Life has seasons, and you can discern inside you that your life is going into a time of change. You feel a longing, an unfulfilled purpose, or an inner yearning to pursue a higher call; a sense of dissatisfaction with your current circumstances or an enigmatic optimism for your future. The Holy Spirit is working in your heart for a time of change. Life is in a perpetual state of altering circumstances.

This book is about change. The change you are anticipating. The change that you are planning. The change you are hoping to improve your situation. The change you might not realise you are already in. The change God wants to happen in your life. The change in your profession that the Lord can leverage for His purpose. The change that will endanger a stable, enduring, successful career or business you are currently enjoying. Your Heavenly Father might have something for you—an impression that is not what you have pictured in your mind.

When you commit to our Lord Jesus, you have entered into a life-changing relationship with Him and joined a lifelong journey of constant transformation. You are in a continuous adventure of change. In this new life in Christ, through the Holy Spirit, the Father redirects or repurposes your vocation and mission.

In Prosci's **ADKAR Model**[1] on Change Management, *Awareness* is the first step of the process, being *aware* of the CHANGE that is happening around you. An awareness that the circumstances, either great or small, are part of the overall change process and nothing that is happening or has happened or will happen is random or coincidental or as a result of world events. Change is not just a matter of the inadvertent consequences of situations or events falling like autumn leaves.

This book aims to help you gain that awareness of the transformative process happening in your life, similar to what the Heavenly Father did as He guided men and women of faith in the Scriptures. An inner prompting, situational conditions, or surrounding events driving this change. These pages study seven Old and New Testament personalities on how the hand of the Lord influenced and managed each of their transitional phases. In some of these chapters, we will analyse the call narratives they encountered.

These people of faith carry testimonies of love, obedience, humility, and trust. The personal stories I share during the discourse, are not intended to draw parallels between my life and theirs, but to highlight the commonality of their situations and struggles with ours when we examine the circumstances surrounding these events. As Paul has said:

> *"Not that I have already attained, or am already perfected; but I press on, that I may lay hold of that for which Christ Jesus has also laid hold of me. Brethren, I do not count myself to have apprehended; but one thing I do, forgetting those things which are behind and reaching forward to those things which are ahead, I press toward the goal for the prize of the upward call of God in Christ Jesus."*
> – Philippians 3:12-14

---

[1] https://www.prosci.com/methodology/adkar

INTRODUCTION

By faith. Yes, it was by faith that these distinguished men and women confronted the circumstances of their calling and adapted to the required changes. Most of these changes did not come easy, and some even found themselves in these circumstances as a result of external events or situations through no fault of their own. All of God's children are called to this life of faith. You are called to this faith and have your unique personal and precious stories that summate as part of God's bigger plan.

The challenge is not about changing one's current career or job, although that could be on the table, but that the Lord could use any of these transformation cases to talk to you personally about a Christ-centred purpose or vocation.

Dr. David Jeremiah said in his book *Forward*, "God opens and closes doors, arranges circumstances, and sometimes creates trajectories you didn't expect."[2]

Then what will be the consequences of ignoring or avoiding the challenges of change?

First, you will miss out on God's blessings. God wants to bless His children, and God wants to bless you. Are you hindering Him in blessing you? Second, you will lose the opportunity to experience God's miracles in your life. Third, you cannot witness how God fulfils His promises to His children. And finally, you will be left behind on the incredible journey God has laid out for you.

I started this book while trying to understand where my professional life was heading as situations and events unfolded around me. *What are you telling me, Lord?* I prayed, "LORD, *what do you want me to do*?" I studied the Scriptures and journaled how our loving Heavenly Father was purposely and precisely involved in the lives of His children to fulfil His plan. This helped me understand and put into perspective what was happening in my life and the world around me. And how being faithful to the call of Christ contributes to God's

---

[2] Dr. David Jeremiah, "Forward: Discovering God's Presence and Purpose in Your Tomorrow" (Nashville, TN: W Publishing an imprint of Thomas Nelson, 2020) 31

plan. God deals with us individually, yet our life's small contribution is woven together in God's overall plan.

I hope and pray I will have another chance to meditate, research and write on a further seven or more Scriptural personalities and discover how the Lord used their career transitions to further the Gospel.

Out of the 8 billion individuals in the world (2023) and millions more before, how can my minute life, my short stint in a job or career, play a part in God's grand plan for mankind? You can feel minuscule, like a grain of sand on a beach, yet you are precious to Him. He knows you by name. As a shepherd leaves his 99 sheep to focus on the need and precarious situation of one, He has His focused attention on and love for that one precious lamb, YOU. Your life matters to Him, and He will work His loving plan *through* you.

Do you feel that God, through the Holy Spirit, is reaching out to you concerning your current career?

Winter does not last forever. Do not let the long nights and cold dark days of winter prolong their grip. After winter comes spring where new life sprouts forth and flowers bloom with new life. A change in season brings fresh hope.

As you read each chapter of this book, I entreat you to ask questions. How does the principal person in the story relate to you? At the end of each chapter, I have listed questions from my own study which helped me probe deeper, read further, and pray harder. Use these questions to discuss with your friends or churchmates or to dig deeper into the narrative of the Scriptures. Remember, the secrets to a blessed study are the Word of God and a sincere and prayerful seeking heart.

I pray that one or more of these stories will speak to you and that you will be able to relate to their journeys in ways that will prove as helpful for you as they did for me. *"Looking unto Jesus, the author and finisher of our faith."*

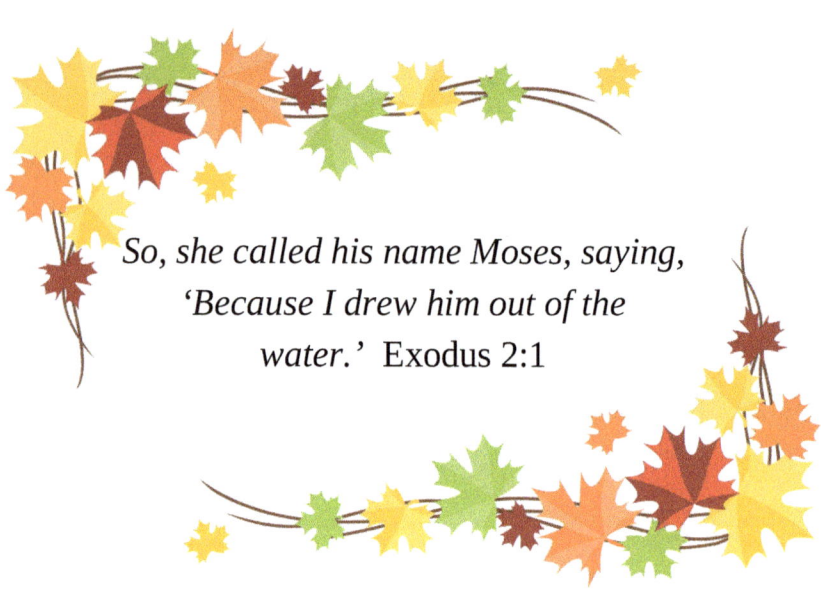

So, she called his name Moses, saying, 'Because I drew him out of the water.' Exodus 2:1

CATALYST OF CHANGE

Drawn Out of the Water

I LOVE MUSIC. I LOVE TO SING. I love to praise and worship my Lord and Saviour, Jesus, especially through singing. I have always been active in serving God in all the churches I have been ascribed to, through the gift of singing which He gave me. This area of ministry has given me great joy and peace. I started singing in the bass section of various choirs but was later assigned to the baritone vocals as well. Singing Handel's Messiah in a choir was the pinnacle of my choral experience, especially giving praise and thanks to Almighty God in the Hallelujah Chorus, *"And He shall reign forever and ever, Amen!"*

I also joined an all-male quartet. Here, I sharpened my singing talent technically by singing together with the other three sections in harmony, joyfully praising God even through challenging broken-chord music pieces! I brought this gift God bestowed on me to my new home church in New Zealand. However, the Lord had different plans.

The church I joined didn't have a formal choir, so I joined a community choral group for a year. Occasionally, our church organised singers for the praise and worship section of a special event. I also volunteered to be a part of the regular roster of backup singers for the Sunday Praise and Worship team. But something seemed wrong. Slowly, I came to realise I couldn't fully exercise my singing gift as I used to. I couldn't blend my voice with the team as I did in the past with the choir or quartet.

Later, I discovered I had tinnitus. At first, I thought crickets were more prevalent in Auckland and more active at night, but after my doctor asked me to undergo a series of hearing tests and ear and head scans, they confirmed I had tinnitus. I believe that at this point, God was *drawing me out* of this area of ministry into using another gifting the Lord has given me, where I had served in several churches before: Children's Ministry, which was always short of male teachers.

This transition opened my heart to hear God's voice prompting me to initiate the formation of a new community outreach for young boys in our church, called BB-ICONZ (related to Boys' Brigade International).

Moses, or מֹשֶׁה (mōšeh), was the name given to an Israelite boy by Pharoah's daughter who *"drew him out of the water,"* out of the River Nile when he was a baby. Similarly, the phrase *drew out*, could also mean removed, taken out, redeemed, pulled out or dragged out.

If we are to examine, like a crime scene, the situation and events leading to Moses' birth and early childhood, the pieces of evidence would all point to Yahweh. The hand of God was directly involved in all the circumstances from before his birth, all the way through to his adoption into the palace of Pharoah.

This is how Moses lived in the Providence of God:

1. **The Promise of God**

   The Lord Yahweh made a covenant with Abraham that He would make him a great nation. After Joseph died, the new Pharoah, who did not know him or what he had done for the kingdom came to power. When the number of Israelites grew, *"and the land was filled with them"*, the new king did not like the foreigners being more significant in number and mightier than the Egyptians. So, Pharoah and his team devised a plan to oppress them with forced labour as a way to control their population boom. But the more the Israelites were oppressed, the more they multiplied, for they became more "fruitful and increased abundantly, multiplied and grew exceedingly mighty."

   John MacArthur said, "The growth of the nation was phenomenal! It grew from 70 men to 603,000 males, 20 years of age and older, thus allowing for a total population of about two million departing from Egypt."[3]

2. The Persecution of the Israelites

Not only were the children of Israel oppressed, but next came one of the darkest days in their history with the murder of newborn males. Pharoah instructed the Hebrew midwives that upon the birth of an Israelite baby, if it was a boy, they should kill it and tell the mother the baby had died during the birthing process. When this plan failed because the midwives feared God more than Pharoah, he instructed that every son born in a Hebrew household must be thrown into the river to drown. This horrific persecution actually helped propel Moses to the highest place in the palace.

3. The Priestly Tribe of Israel

The parents of Moses, Jochebed and Amram (Exodus 6:20), were both members of the family of Levi. Levites were to become the tribe responsible for the religious leadership of the children of Israel. Therefore, Moses was predestined to be a priest for His people.

4. The Protection of God

It was in the midst of one of humanity's most gruesome infanticides that the Lord's power of protection was manifested. He spread His hand over His chosen servant, who would eventually lead His people out of Egypt. Moses was shielded from the massacre of Jewish baby boys. When Jochebed saw her baby boy was beautiful, she went against Pharoah's edict and hid him. Then, when the babies were being thrown into the Nile River, she instead placed Moses in an ark of bulrushes before floating

---

[3] MacArthur Study Bible, Copyright © 1997, 2006, 2019 by Thomas Nelson. All rights reserved.

him on the river. It was here that Pharoah's daughter found and rescued him from the murderous orders of her father.

In God's providence, this boy was raised in the ways of Yahweh, as he was nurtured and brought up by a Hebrew nurse, who just happened to be his real mother. And all the expenses of his upbringing were paid for by the daughter of Pharoah!

5. The Pathway to the Palace

To have the right person with the qualities and skillset to lead God's people out of bondage in Egypt to the promised land, Moses needed to be equipped with the leadership and management skills, and knowledge of the kingdom of Egypt. Surviving the massacre was not sufficient, but through God's providence, the compassion of Pharoah's daughter for a crying baby left in the river, gave Moses a 'scholarship grant' where he became *"learned in all the wisdom of the Egyptians, and was mighty in words and deeds."* Acts 7:22

Just as the Lord's providence was towards Moses, God's hand is also directly involved in all the events and circumstances in our lives. The Scripture proclaims the promises He has for His children. We may be persecuted and rejected because we are followers of Jesus. In the same way, we may encounter unfavourable or unpleasant situations in our lives. But as children of the Most-High, we are all called into a royal priesthood (I Peter 2:9), and His almighty hand will protect us as He establishes our feet in the path of His plan (Psalm 37:23-24).

The Providence of God continues to impact the rest of Moses' life. When a lover of Scripture observes his life, they will see a literary rhythmic downbeat occurring. As they zoom out and observe the timeline of his life, they will see the pattern. This is how beautiful and metrical the timing is at the stroke of the Lord's baton.

Then his career changed dramatically, and in rhythmic events every forty years. As the great evangelist and writer, Dwight L. Moody, said:

Moses spent forty years thinking he was somebody,
forty years learning he was nobody,
and forty years discovering
what God can do with a nobody.

Here is an overview of the life of Moses:

Age	Period	Exodus	Scenario
0-40	Life in Egypt	Chapter 2	Birth in Egypt but nursed by a Hebrew
			First 40 years of Moses' life
			Egyptian Monarchy
			Egyptian Education
			Worked in Pharoah's court
Trigger: Moses killed and buried an Egyptian beating a Hebrew brother. He was exposed for this crime.			
40-80	Life in Midian	Chapter 3	Flee to neighbouring Midian
			Settled and started a family
			Tending the flock of Reuel Priest of Midian (a.k.a. Jethro)
			Worked for Jethro and married one of his daughters
Trigger: God appeared and talked to Moses through a burning bush			
80-120	Life in the Wilderness	Chapters 4+	Moses went back to Egypt
			Moses demanded Pharoah to let his people go
			Moses released God's judgement to Egypt
			Moses led God's people out of Egypt to the Promised Land

Drawn Out of Royalty
Exodus 2:1-15
Acts 7:17-29
Hebrews 11:23-28

For 33 years, Karl Bohnak worked at his dream job, delivering weather forecasts on TV for what he considered one of the most challenging but beautiful spots in the United States — Michigan's Upper Peninsula.

He became so popular, the saying, "That's what Karl says!" became a slogan at his station in the 1990s and even inspired a song.

But Bohnak's time as chief meteorologist for news station TV6 came to an abrupt end. He was fired after refusing to comply with the vaccine mandate imposed by his station's corporate owner, Gray Television.

"I just did not want to take the shot," says Bohnak, who is 68. "I felt it was my right as a human being and a citizen of the U.S. to decide what I put in my body."[4]

This story was repeated by others, becoming a reality when they decided according to their conscience and sincere belief that they could not accept vaccination. Consequently, they found their employment endangered and even terminated. They were forced to leave their beloved career to pursue a different profession, or go into business for themselves.

The first career change Moses underwent was triggered when he decided to kill an Egyptian taskmaster. *"For he supposed that his brethren would have understood that God would deliver them by his hand, but they did not understand."* (Acts 7:25) He made a conscious decision in the name of justice, and that action changed the course of his career in the palace.

In his story, here are the points leading to this change.

---

[4] Andrea Hsu, "Thousands of workers are opting to get fired, rather than take the vaccine." https://www.npr.org/2021/10/24/1047947268/covid-vaccine-workers-quitting-getting-fired-mandates

6. **Patriotic and Proud of His heritage**

   In the midst of a mass killing of baby boys of Israeli descent, his life was spared and sheltered by the sovereign hand of God, using Pharoah's daughter to protect him from the wrath of her father. Then he was entrusted to his actual mother to be nursed and raised, and taught regarding his heritage, culture, traditions and, more importantly, how to love and trust Yahweh. A person's formative years are the time when they establish their values and beliefs. Moses knew he was a Hebrew and not an Egyptian. He knew Yahweh God, and the Lord knew him by name.

   We must value our distinct culture, heritage, and traditions. These are the spirit of our identity as a person and as a cultural group. Above all, we must uphold the Christian statutes and values on which our forefathers built this country and raised their families.

7. **Premier Education**

   God opened the door for Moses to gain access to the best education and training the country of Egypt offered, if not the best in the known world. As the son of Pharoah's daughter, he was instructed in every subject to the highest standard for that day and time. The best teachers, scientists, mathematicians, philosophers, military artisans, and tacticians were at his disposal in this exclusive school, just like Joseph, who had access as second in command in the kingdom. What more could be asked for to gain the qualifications to deliver the children of Israel out of Egypt?

   Moses had a grand opportunity to learn from the best the land of Egypt had to offer in terms of education and experience.

8. **Proponent of Justice**

   Moses had such an inherent passion for justice, *"that he went out to his brethren and looked at their burdens."* (Exodus 2:11) And because of this personality trait, he triggered the process of career change in his life. He reacted instinctively when he saw one of his brethren being beaten by an Egyptian taskmaster, which ended tragically.

Later, Moses faced another incident of injustice when he encountered a group of maidens being bullied by some shepherds, stealing water for their flocks which they did not draw. In that situation, Moses ended up with a more favourable outcome.

When the Lord created you, He endowed you with a personality which is uniquely different to all His other creations. He has His reasons why you are extroverted, or shy, or sporty, or nerdy. The personality you have will react differently to other followers of Christ, even when you are encountering the same situation. We should thank our Creator for our unique personality and pray He will fully leverage our lives for His plan and glory.

9. Personal Decisions

A former president of the United States once told Vanity Fair what he did to help him make important decisions every day when he was in office:

> *"You'll see I wear only gray or blue suits,"* [Obama] *said. "I'm trying to pare down decisions. I don't want to make decisions about what I'm eating or wearing. Because I have too many other decisions to make."*

When I learnt this technique, I took this principle and applied it to my daily routine, but with a unique twist. I make it a point to decide on and prepare the clothes I wear to the office the night before. This eliminates the pressure or cluttered decision-making of what to wear, especially when late or rushing to get the car or train in the morning rush.

> *"So teach us to number our days,*
> *That we may gain a heart of wisdom."*
> Psalm 90:12

This is a Psalmist's prayer to our loving Heavenly Father to help us make the right decisions every time, every day, and that they correspondingly align with His perfect will for us. We should treat all decisions as spiritual decisions, whether the spirituality of the matter is explicit or not.

Moses decided to step out from his silo in the palace to see the welfare of his people. He also decided to rescue his fellow Hebrew from the abuse and cruelty of a taskmaster, which ultimately impacted his future. Was it the right decision or not? At that moment it seemed to him that his sense of justice resulted in a horrible decision, but when looking in hindsight at the life of Moses, this fits perfectly into God's big picture.

Pray daily that the Lord will guide us in all the decisions we make.

10. Passion for His People

Even during the years as he grew up under the Egyptian educational system, walking on the grounds of the central governing institution and rubbing shoulders with the 'who's who' in Egyptian society, Moses knew who he was, a Hebrew, a descendant of Abraham, Isaac, and Jacob.

> *"Now when he was forty years old, it came into his heart to visit his brethren, the children of Israel."*
> Acts 7:23

He had a passion for his people, the Israelites… someone who cared about the welfare of his people. He stepped outside the protected realm of the Egyptian palace walls and into the workplace of his people. As Oliver Wendell Holmes, Sr., a physician and poet, and father of the supreme court justice, wrote:

> *"Some people are so heavenly minded that they are no earthly good."*

We have to step out of our Christian comfort-zone to go out and reach people with the Gospel of Christ.

11. Proclivity for Self-Preservation

Moses only realised he was already in a profession-changing process when he discovered there were others who knew what he had done to the Egyptian taskmaster. This became his moment of *change awareness*.

When he decided to defend a brother from an oppressor, he shut the doors to all possibility of normality in his life. Thinking that no one was there to witness his premeditated action, he was surprised to learn otherwise when he tried to help settle a conflict between two Hebrews.

When Pharoah heard what Moses had done to one of his taskmasters, he ordered Moses to be killed. This automatically triggered Moses' self-preservation mode, an instinctively inherent part of all humanity, created in us by God. That is, we nourish, protect, and heal our bodies as our primary biological function. Maslow's *Hierarchy of Needs* shows that physiological and safety needs are the first two levels of need that dictate an individual's behaviour[5]. Moses fled Egypt and went to a neighbouring country called Midian. This instinctive characteristic of self-preservation caused the next part in the chain reaction of this process of change.

I could not help but recall the prayer of Jesus to His Father in heaven at the lowest point of His emotions, when He contemplated His imminent suffering and death on the cross. This prayer displayed His full humanity.

> *"Father, if you are willing, take this cup from me; yet not my will, but yours be done."*
> Luke 22:42

Several men and women of God have acted from their human instinct. Acts of self-preservation or human compassion, righteous anger or expressions of love, doubt, or faith, are inherent in

---

[5] Maslow's hierarchy of needs: https://en.wikipedia.org/wiki/Maslow%27s_hierarchy_of_needs

all individuals because we are *human*, the most loved creation of God. And all the more should we surrender these to be controlled by His Spirit.

12. The Posture of an Officer and a Gentleman

> *"An officer is, from his position, a leader of men. He must show in himself such qualities as he desires to bring out in those under his leadership. A gentleman is exactly what the word signifies, a gentle man.*
>
> *"In the Government Articles for the Navy the following words are found:*
>
> *"'The commanders of all fleets, squadrons, naval stations, and vessels belonging to the navy are required to show, in themselves, a good example of virtue, honor, patriotism, and subordination.'*
>
> *"The possession of these four fundamental qualities—as they may be called—will produce neither an officer nor a gentleman in the fullest sense of the words. To them must be added initiative, ambition, loyalty, good judgment, and justice, together with a certain human kindness all cemented with an unfailing sense of courtesy and tact."*
> – *Lieutenant (j.g.) H.E. Dow, U.S.N.R.F.*[6]

As Moses fled from Egypt for his life, he sat and rested from his long and tiring journey at a *well*, where thirst-quenching crystal waters would cool down his wearied body. A group of ladies came to the well and filled the troughs to give water to their flock. Suddenly, a group of shepherds arrived and bullied the ladies out of the way to let their own flocks drink from the pre-

---

[6] THE TRUE MEANING OF THE PHRASE "AN OFFICER AND A GENTLEMAN" https://www.usni.org/magazines/proceedings/1922/december/true-meaning-phrase-officer-and-gentleman

filled troughs. In his sense of justice, this person seeming to be Egyptian sitting by the well, stood up, drove the invading shepherds away and helped the ladies continue watering their flocks. Moses used his royal training in Pharoah's courts to achieve this feat, a true act of an Officer and a Gentleman!

Reuel, the priest of Midian, the owner of the flock the ladies were tending, noticed his daughters coming home earlier than usual. This led me to conclude this bullying scene was a recurring incident. Moses was a blessing to the family of Reuel. This time, his sense of justice brought him favour in the eyes of Reuel. His training in Egypt of being an Officer and a Gentleman had served him well.

Sometimes, people will misinterpret, misunderstand, misread, or assume you are someone you are not, especially during the process of change, just as Moses was identified as an Egyptian. But God knows who you are and what you are capable of, and that your inherent and learned character will come out and be utilised at the right moment to fulfil His purpose for you. The Lord Almighty will definitely leverage all your talents, skills, education, and training for His overall plan for you and His kingdom, especially when He is the one who lets you experience them first. We need to let Him take control.

13. Pleasant Manners

Moses courteously accepted the hospitality of Reuel, also known as Jethro, who prepared a dinner in gratitude to Moses for helping his daughters, as well as being a customary gesture to travelling strangers. This courteous attitude helped Moses adapt to his new environment, new country and eventually, a new family.

My mum used to remind me to "always mind your manners" whenever I went to a friend's house or a birthday party. As a guest, good manners is the least you can give your generous host for taking the time and effort to set things up and invite YOU, and having you as an honoured guest. A good and gracious manner is our expression of appreciation and respect to the host for the generosity given.

14. Profound Humility

Moses was content and agreed to stay permanently with Jethro. He was physically and mentally settled in his new environment, and God gave him peace in this new life. Later, his sentiments were further established in Midian when Reuel gave his daughter, Zipporah, to be Moses' wife who became the mother of his son, Gershom, which means *stranger*.

> *"I have been a stranger in a foreign land."*
> Exodus 2:22b

From the height of palace life, he humbly accepted his new circumstances in this new country, away from his royal standing in Egypt. Humility is an essential trait when one is undergoing change; humility to let go of firmly held lifestyles, attitudes, achievements, and positions; realising that *"old things have passed away; behold, all things have become new."* (II Corinthians 5:17B)

Drawn Out of Obscurity

When the second career change came to Moses, the Lord Yahweh Himself initiated the change. Moses had been *"...tending the flock of Jethro his father-in-law, the priest of Midian"* (Exodus 3:1) for 40 years. He was away from life in the metropolis of Egypt, where city life was bustling with people chatting and shouting, with the boisterously loud voices of the marketplace, with the flamboyant and outlandish colours of clothes and jewellery. Here in Midian, he lived a tranquil country life by the mountainside and desert where the only noises he had to deal with was the bleating of his flock, day after day, year after year. No one knew, not even Moses himself, that something big was about to happen in his 80th year.

In those forty years, he had settled down in Midian with a wonderful wife and two sons. And every day, he tended and watched his father-in-law's livestock grow. He had a quiet and manageable life as he grew to a ripe age.

However, God had other things planned for Moses – every moment of his life, his career development plan can be attributed to God's timetable.

Chapter three of Exodus sets the scene for this encounter. The day was just another ordinary day in the workplace for Moses, letting the flock graze on a field by the mountainside, then quench their thirst from the water by the well… a typical day in his forty years as a shepherd. But this specific day, was going to be different. It was the day that changed, once again, the course and career of Moses' life.

While Moses was passing by Mt. Sinai with his flock as he usually did, something very unusual caught his attention. It was a burning bush, but very strangely, this bush was not being consumed by the flames. A miracle was happening right before his eyes. What a way to get one's attention in a very mundane life! Curiosity got the best of Moses.

> *"So when the Lord saw that he turned aside to look,*
> *God called to him from the midst of the bush and*
> *said, 'Moses, Moses!'"*

God called out to Moses *by name*! When you hear your name out of thin air, that will surely disrupt the monotony of your work cycle.

For, "A person's name is to that person the sweetest and most important sound in any language."[7] – Dale Carnegie

"Carnegie explains that if you want to get someone's attention, use their name."[8] – Dr Roger Moore

Moses responded, *"Here I am."*

---

[7] Dale Carnegie from *How to Win Friends and Influence People*.
[8] Dr Roger Moore from *DermacenterMD*

God wanted to have a conversation with Moses about his future, and He wants to have one with you too, but maybe not as grandiose as His plans for Moses. He *will* initiate that conversation.

In this discourse between God and Moses, God laid out His plan for His people in Egypt. Moses was again *drawn out*, but this time to lead this new project.

As the burning bush incident unfolds, we will discover important points, not only about the conversation, but also about what attributes a man or woman of God should have.

1. Working Hands, not Idle Hands

Idle hands are not what God wants for His children, even in a time of waiting or training.

> *"He who has a slack hand becomes poor,*
> *But the hand of the diligent makes rich."*
> Proverbs 10:4

> *"Because of laziness the building decays,*
> *And through idleness of hands the house leaks."*
> Ecclesiastes 10:18

Moses was busy tending the flock of his father-in-law when an Angel of the Lord got his attention. He was not purposely looking for a sign from Yahweh, nor was he sitting idly waiting for instructions.

An experienced driver once told me, *"It is easier to turn the steering wheel when a car is moving rather than in a stand-still position."* So, a person who is active or busy doing something, working, volunteering, etc., is quicker to engage in God's action-packed plan for His kingdom than an idle one.

Do not stop working or being productive; God will set a meeting schedule in your busy diary.

2. Sensitive to His Gentle Whisper

Moses did not get a 'big, loud voice in the sky' introduction to the change in his career; rather, his attention was caught out of the corner of his eye by a *burning bush* along the mundane path where he usually led his flock. Curiosity may have killed a cat. However, Moses' curiosity led him to one of the most significant revelations in his life.

> *"I will now turn aside and see this great sight, why the bush does not burn."* Exodus 3:3

Not everyone needs a burning bush, especially not if you demand one. Nevertheless, you must be observant of the things around you. I believe that when God wants to speak to you or reveal something to you, He will do it in a way that will get your attention. It may come in the slightest and gentlest whisper, or a devastating heartbreak. You need to abide in Him (John 15), so you will know His voice (John 10).

Recently, in 2022, I was assigned to lead the Bible story segment of my church's Sunday School. I was scheduled for the third week of the term. One of our team's storytellers needed to swap her assigned week, so I volunteered; I preferred to complete my duties early so I could focus more on the physically demanding boys' ministry. The Bible story character for that week was Elijah. As I was doing my usual research and meditation, I asked the Holy Spirit how I should present this message, and here is one of several messages I received from the Lord:

> *"The Lord said, 'Go out and stand on the mountain in the presence of the Lord, for the Lord is about to pass by.'*
>
> *Then a great and powerful wind tore the mountains apart and shattered the rocks before the Lord, but the Lord was not in the wind. After the wind there was an earthquake, but the Lord was not in the*

> *earthquake. After the earthquake came a fire, but the Lord was not in the fire. And after the fire came a gentle whisper. When Elijah heard it, he pulled his cloak over his face and went out and stood at the mouth of the cave.*
>
> *Then a voice said to him,*
> *'What are you doing here, Elijah?'"*
> I Kings 19:11-13

God's voice and message can come to you in a *gentle whisper*. The all-knowing, all-powerful, and ever-present God can come to you in a soft, kind voice. A voice you can trust and feel secure in.

Be mindful of the things around you. You must be aware of when the Lord may personally reach out for one-on-one interaction with you in the midst of your present-day busyness and distractions. However, you should also be mindful not to overreact, as if anything and everything has a message. *'Pray continually…'* (I Thessalonians 5:17)

3. When God Speaks

"God called to him from the midst of the bush and said, 'Moses, Moses!'" (Exodus 3:4) Jesus knows you, and He will call you by name. How do you respond when someone calls you by your name? Jesus is your friend, and you must expect He will treat you as such when He talks to you. Do you recognise His voice when He calls for you? Our God is a personal God.

> *"So, the Lord spoke to Moses face to face, as a man speaks to his friend." Exodus 33:11*

Moses said, *"Here I am."* (Exodus 3:4). Avoiding the conversation is not the proper way to respond to the Lord. When our Saviour calls your 'mobile', we should never *decline* the call.

Jonah tried to *ghost* God and reject his Nineveh assignment, but he ended up having a big fish as his special mode of transport.

Samuel followed what the Prophet Eli told him to do when he kept hearing his name being called in the middle of the night, *"Speak, Lord, for your servant is listening."* 1 Samuel 3:9

In Isaiah 6:8, the discourse between God and Isaiah reveals the attitude we must pursue:

> *"Also, I heard the voice of the Lord, saying,*
> *'Whom shall I send,*
> *And who will go for Us?'*
> *Then I said, 'Here am I! Send me.'"*

Moses heard his name audibly and replied, *"Here I am."*

> **Prayer Point**
> *The mobile phone of your heart may be ringing now.*
> *Is God on the line? Go ahead and answer His call.*
> *Have that sweet time conversing with your Saviour,*
> *the Lover of our soul!*

4. When We Become Aware, We Respond in Reverence

"Then He said, 'Do not draw near this place. Take your sandals off your feet, for the place where you stand is holy ground.'" (Exodus 3:5) Moses did not let his previous royal pride stand in the way of his conversation with God. He knew his place in this universe. Maybe 40 years with the sheep had weaned his concept of royalty from his mental system. Realising who had just talked to him through the burning bush, Moses reacted with his whole being to the presence and personality of the Speaker, the God of Abraham, Isaac and Israel, the patriarchs of the Hebrew nation. His reaction was one of worship and surrender. He bowed in worship to the Creator of all things. God *will* constantly remind

us to be humble in His presence. When we talk to God, we do not raise our heads but prostrate our hearts.

5. Listening Intently

Moses listened to hear the reason God was calling him. God's mission for Moses was the monumental task of leading the Israelites out of Egypt and into the promised land. He needed to know the reason in order to gain a resolute conviction of his mission. The case the Lord stated once again elicited Moses' sense of justice for the oppressed.

God will present His case for you to act upon, based on the character and personality He has created in you since conception (Psalm 139).

6. Evaluate Yourself Honestly

Author Paul Este, wrote about The Half-Life of Skills[9] in big tech organisations, where he states that the half-life of the skills you have learned today is *five years!* Therefore, an organisation's top People and Capability priority should greatly emphasise re-skilling their workforce.

After 40 years away from the Egyptian empire, tending sheep and goats, his court skills and administration abilities would have dramatically diminished, but not been totally eliminated.

If you have been out of the workplace for a while, you may doubt your knowledge and ability to do business. However, sometimes this is what God needs from His children, their total reliance on the Master.

When God sends you, He does so with His blessing and assurances! When you doubt your ability to complete a task or to pursue a call, it is spiritually natural to question your human frailty, but the Holy Spirit will ALWAYS remind you of His promises.

The Lord said, "I will certainly be with you." Exodus 3:12

---

[9] https://hrdailyadvisor.blr.com/2020/03/25/the-half-life-of-skills/

God does not rely on man's strengths and abilities, nor should His children. We should rely on God. On His power and His promises.

7. Walking with Authority

"I AM WHO I AM."

Moses remembered his lack of authority when two fighting Hebrews challenged him. "WHO made you a prince and judge over us?" (Exodus 2:14) Moses asked God, "Indeed, when I come to the children of Israel and say to them, 'The God of your fathers has sent me to you,' and they say to me, 'What is His name?' what shall I say to them?" (Exodus 3:13)

God replied, "I AM WHO I AM."

There is a short clip from the Bible Project on Yahweh – Lord.[10] They presented a word study on the name of the LORD, which provides a good background understanding to this event. Likewise, here is another exciting video on Richard Rohr's YHWH.[11]

As 21st-century Christians, we should remember and dwell in the powerful promise of the Great Commission given by our Lord Jesus:

> *"All authority has been given to Me in heaven and on earth. Go therefore and make disciples of all the nations, baptizing them in the name of the Father and of the Son and of the Holy Spirit, teaching them to observe all things that I have commanded you; and lo, I am with you always, even to the end of the age."*
> Matthew 28:18-20

---

[10] Bible Project on Yahweh – Lord: https://youtu.be/eLrGM26pmM0
[11] Richard Rohr's YHWH: https://www.youtube.com/watch?v=SilgjFpdtwM

8. Reality of Resistance

When you start a ministry to propagate the gospel, you will most certainly come under attack from the enemy. When you raise the banner of the Cross, you are conquering the territory of the evil one, and the enemy will not just stand there idle and let you walk over him. You should even question the assignment if it is not met with challenges that require stretching your faith, or sending you to your knees to pray. Expect challenges, expect opposition, and be steadfast and sure. Moses encountered much resistance, from the people of Israel all the way up to the Pharoah of Egypt. This is the most realistic expectation, and you must anticipate it when taking on God's work.

In his book, *The Prayer of Jabez,* Bruce Wilkinson shared a story about when his mentor, Professor Howard Hendricks, was talking to one of his students who was excited to tell the professor how well his life was going.

"When I first came here," the student said, *"I was so tempted and tested I could barely keep my head above water. But now – Praise God! – my life at seminary has smoothed out. I'm not being tempted hardly at all!"*

But Hendricks looked deeply alarmed – not the reaction the student was expecting. "That's about the worst thing I could have heard." He told the surprised senior, "That shows me that you're no longer in the battle! Satan isn't worried about you anymore."[12]

9. What Do You Have?

Assigned with this tremendous task, God had already provided Moses with all that he NEEDED to accomplish this charge: **God's Word**. However, Moses was still human and raised a counter-argument. What if the people challenged him on whether God really had appeared to him? He was asking God what

---

[12] Dr Bruce H. Wilkinson, The Prayer of Jabez. Multnomah Publishers, 2000

physical evidence he had to prove God had spoken to him, not just a verbal confirmation. Man is obsessed with seeing and feeling something from the divine universe before concluding that the spiritual world exists. Time and time again, pieces of evidence appear proving that the Scriptures are true. However, these will never be enough for some people. The Lord asked Moses, *"What is that in your hand?"* Just like the boy who offered his lunch of five loaves and two fish to Jesus, when the Lord asks, *"How many loaves do you have? Go and see."* (Mark 6:38) Even without this heavenly revelation, Moses already had what he physically needed to show and convince the people of Israel that God had appeared to him. He only needed to let God work through him, through his faith.

10. Importance of Communication

In this age of misinformation, disinformation and fact-checkers, communication is vital. Humans control the masses through communication, and Moses knew this. Eloquence and deflection are the modern world's power, but Christians should never forget that it is the Lord's Spirit who changes men's hearts. Moses missed that critical ingredient in ministry; he needed to be reminded again that the Holy Spirit is the One working.

> *"Then Moses said to the Lord,*
> *'O my Lord, I am not eloquent,*
> *neither before nor since You have spoken to Your*
> *servant; but I am slow of speech and slow of tongue.'*

> *"So the Lord said to him, 'Who has made man's*
> *mouth? Or who makes the mute, the deaf, the seeing,*
> *or the blind? Have not I, the Lord? Now therefore,*
> *go, and I will be with your mouth and teach you what*
> *you shall say.'"* Exodus 4:10-12

In His anger towards Moses' doubt, the Lord then assigned his brother, Aaron, to be his Public Relations Officer.

11. Godly Self-Confidence

After all God's promises, Moses still did not believe in himself. This was not due to humility, but more of self-pity. This sin could be mistaken for a godly character, but it is not. The loss of confidence in himself revealed his loss of faith in God, the Creator of his being, and the loss of power that can be achieved through Him and the promises of His Word.

"But Moses said, 'Pardon your servant, Lord. Please send someone else.'" (Exodus 3:13) Here, Moses showed his resistance to this latest career change. He did not feel adequate for his new assignment and thought someone else might be better for the job. God did not make a mistake. He knew Moses, and He wanted him for this assignment.

Abigail Dodds wrote, *"The sin in self-pity is that we assess ourselves and our circumstances as though God is not our gracious Father.*

"The problem of self-pity is a problem of sight. Self-pitying people have not set the Lord before themselves as he really is — glorious, kind, sovereign, and just. They mainly have set themselves and their circumstances in their field of vision. Rather than crying out to God in our big and small moments of distress, self-pity would have us whimper in the misery of our own hearts."[13]

The attitude of positive and godly self-confidence is required in ministry. To gain this, we have to remind ourselves how and why God created us, why He saved us, and rely solely on the strength and promises of our Lord in all our tasks.

---

[13] Abigail Dodds, Woe Is Me: The Sin of Self-Pity and How to Be Free, https://www.desiringgod.org/articles/woe-is-me

12. Absolute Submission

The Lord's anger burned against Moses! Despite all the assurances and promises the Lord had given to Moses, he still pleaded to be excused from this calling.

He was comfortable at home in Midian. However, a divine call to change will, most of the time, cause a seismic quake in one's life and family.

At the age of 80, Moses may have some 'plausible' excuses running through his mind NOT to commit to this assignment:

- A significant life change at 80 was not ideal, and he was no longer capable of the tasks.
- He had been taking it slow in his career, just tending the flock, which for him, was suitable for his retirement years.
- Uprooting his family at this late age would be stressful. Imagine moving house at an age when you are able to retire, not to a retirement home but into a nerve-racking career.
- Foreseeable stress—Pharoah, Egyptians, Hebrew leaders, Israelites, travel logistics.
- Learning new things at 80 can be more challenging with a very steep learning curve.
- Physical limitation—why not let a younger man do it?
- Too wise to believe he still has the skills to wield influence in Egypt.

God answered all the excuses given by Moses not to proceed with his mission. This should have removed all the obstacles to going forward with the changes in Moses' life.

We may give a convincing list of reasons to God why we CANNOT, but He will make sure you will be either in His most ideal scenario or the least. At the end of it all, the plan will come to pass.

Let us aspire to witness God's greatness through us.

Section Summary

A Life Story

In my younger years, during my university days, a Christian brother shared with me that he was earnestly praying to God to reveal Himself to him through a burning bush. I truly understood his faith and the plea, and the reasons he wanted such a situation to occur in his life. That would secure the answers to all his questions, for I knew the difficulties and struggles he had and the burdens he was bearing. Could God respond to his request? I told him God could do anything He wished. Would He do it for him? I think God wouldn't.

The Lord is a personal God and relates to His children personally. Most, if not all God-encounters with His children are unique to themselves. These events are recorded NOT to serve as a *template* of a God-experience scenario but as a testimony that the Almighty God communicates and interacts with those who believe and love Him. Insisting on the same miracle is like telling God what to do. God knows how to reach us. We do not set the terms, He does. The Scripture has shown us different ways our Lord has communicated to His children, and His only requirement is for us to trust and obey Him. The relationship will lead to the encounter.

Like Moses, you could also be **drawn out** from your present or future circumstances by our Heavenly Father to a new career, job, profession, business, or to ministry. If you truly want to seek God's will and what He wants you to do for His Kingdom, you know that the security and satisfaction you feel now is just a passing phase. Maybe you are now experiencing that *gentle whisper* from our Lord telling you to go in a different direction.

Section Questions

1. Would you also attribute human-initiated or self-inflicted circumstances to prompt a career change as divine? How and why?

2. Do you think there were other options for Moses to bring retribution or judgement to the Egyptian for beating a Hebrew,

something that would not seal his fate? Would you take that option if you were Moses?

3. How would you act when the direction of your career is beyond your control? For example, when the circumstances around you are determining your future professional or business plans.

4. Recall the event narrated in the Scriptures when Moses stopped by the well in Midian. What did the well mean to Moses? Have you gone to your well? What is your well?

5. List down Bible incidents where the life of a believer or follower of God goes against the instinct of self-preservation; rather than running away for fear for their lives, they faced the consequences or wrath of the authorities.

6. Have you gone through more than one career change in your life? Describe what made you decide to change careers. What prompted you to consider changing jobs or professions or starting a new business?

7. Have you felt that God is trying to start a conversation with you, but you let the busyness drown out that sweet voice? What do you think would be the best method for our Heavenly Father to contact you personally to discuss these matters? Recall an event in the past when the Lord talked to you that led to a significant decision.

8. Write down some general and some specific personal promises the Spirit has prompted you with. Reflect on these passages as you contemplate this decision of change.

9. What is that in your hand? What do you have with you or in you to serve the Lord and for Him to use?

10. What are the reasons stopping you from starting the career change process when you know God is telling you to do so?

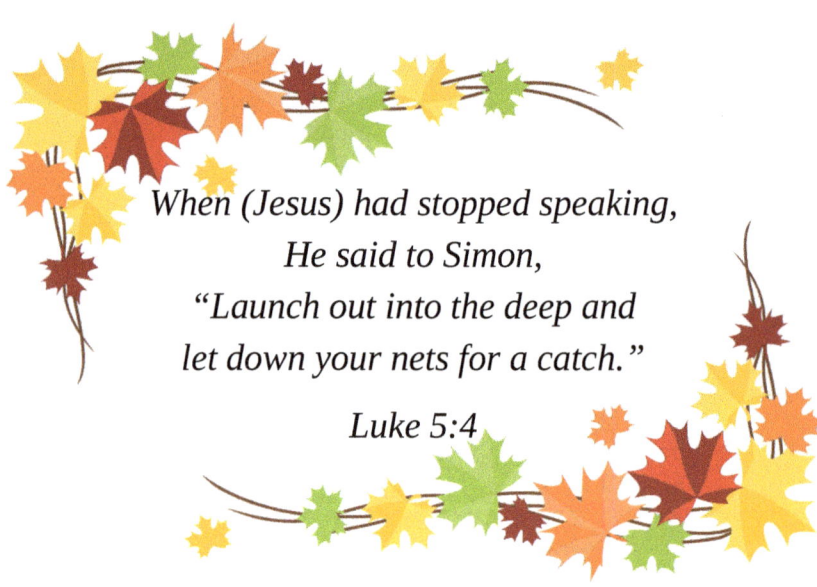

When (Jesus) had stopped speaking,
He said to Simon,
"Launch out into the deep and
let down your nets for a catch."

Luke 5:4

Professional Paralysis

The Rut that Stopped the Best in the Business

HAVE YOU EVER WONDERED how our Lord Jesus would approach you to convince you to change your career, profession or business?

In the New Testament, people often underwent a change in their lifelong profession after their encounter with Him.

Let us now look at how Simon was confronted with a career change.

One evening, Simon, Andrew, James and John went out at dusk, expecting a rewarding haul of fish from an all-night business venture.

These seasoned fishermen knew the best time and location to get a couple of good, full nets, for they had undertaken their trade apprenticeship from none other than the best. To take a closer look, Simon was originally from Bethsaida, a fishermen's city on the eastern bank of the Jordan River. He then settled in Capernaum with his wife and family.

Simon and Andrew, sons of Jonah, and James and John, sons of Zebedee, were professional fishermen in their own right. It was a family business with multigenerational experience tagged to their resume. To them, this activity was just another day at the office and looked like a productive one at that.

But this night, things did not turn out as they planned. The sea was calm and the surroundings were silent. The moon could have shone brightly and clearly through the waters for the fish to see their supper. But none were swimming into the fishing mesh. They pulled up their nets, moved to a new location, and dropped them again. This took place throughout the night; maybe they would have dropped some of their own snacks to bait these aquatic vertebrates. Still, they did not catch any fish! Maybe a piece of seaweed or two, but not a single fish.

With their sleep-deprived eyes and net-etched fingers, you can imagine how downcast their countenances would have been when they came out from that long night's work with empty nets. An unproductive night, with not even a spare catch to alleviate their hunger. Can you relate to these young men? Have you worked long hours to the best of your ability and yet, come out short, empty, or unproductive by your own standards and your superiors'? Have you been running your business at the top of your skills and with all the modern technologies and techniques, but when you looked at the balance of your books at fiscal year-end, the earnings were not worth the effort and investment? Are you trying to resolve a digital-based problem, utilising every bit of knowledge you learned, using all the research and Googling (now using AI), asking all present and past colleagues and mentors for solutions, even putting in many extra hours trying to solve the bug or fault in the system, and still come up with nothing?

The sun's rays started to break through the deepest part of the night, crawling up the horizon, indicating morning had come. The weary fishermen finally realised their venture had been a failure. But life goes on, and as the fireball projected its full glory on their skin, they still needed to complete their business cycle whether they caught plenty or none. When they reached the shore, they wearily dragged their tired bodies and empty nets up the beach to spread them out to dry. They untangled the crossed threads and removed any sea-debris clinging to the lines on each grid as if mocking them and emphasising their failure. They experienced that night that life was cruel and had turned against them.

Since daybreak, a teacher, a Rabbi, had been instructing a crowd at the lakeside while they cleaned their nets. Jesus, the teacher, got into Simon's boat and asked him to put it out a little from the land. This was a practical example of how to manage crowds in a public speaking environment. Making enough room between speaker and audience allows the sound to flow through the open space before reaching the listening ears rather than talking within a crowd and muffling the spoken words. Jesus intentionally used Simon's boat to connect with him, to start a conversation and show him His glory.

After Jesus addressed his audience, He turned His attention to Simon. Jesus told him, *"Launch out into the deep and let down your nets for a catch."*

Simon looked at Jesus in bewilderment, thinking, 'What are you talking about? Who are you? What do you know about fishing? This is not the right time to fish! Do you have any idea what we have gone through this WHOLE NIGHT? We are the experienced ones, the professionals, expert fishermen here, not you! There is nothing! No fish! And, by the way, as you can see, we were about to call it a day as we have almost finished washing out the nets.'

But even with all these objections shouting in Simon's mind, he took a very long, deep breath and responded with resignation and angst: *"Master, we have toiled all night and caught nothing; nevertheless, at Your word I will let down the net."*

Are you presently experiencing a similar obstacle? Is our Lord talking to you in a time of frustration, solitude and surrender in your profession, business, or career? Is this the moment Jesus can have that *conversation* with you to show His glory? Has He asked you to cast your net into the sea to catch fish, or is there something else the Lord has asked you to do at this point for Him?

"…nevertheless, at Your word I will let down the net."

'Here goes my reputation.' Simon may have talked to himself again saying, 'What am I doing with all these people staring at me—watching stupid me listening to this street-preacher-carpenter, after I had failed and caught NOTHING? Here goes!'

SPLASH!

Suddenly, schools of fish miraculously appeared in Simon's net! 'Where have these fish come from?' he may have thought. He and

Andrew tried pulling in their nets, 'Whoa, too heavy! Our boat is tipping over, and the net is starting to rip!'

He shouted to his mates, "James! John! We need help here! The nets are too full, and the boat is about to go over!" So, the brothers came with their boat to help Simon and Andrew, and they filled both boats! So full, the boats almost started to sink.

What a blessing! Did Simon specifically ask Jesus for this blessing, that after a night of fishless nets, to get two overfilled fishing boats? Did Simon and his fishing buddies deserve such a blessing? Simon, Andrew, James and John were explicitly targeted for this miracle, which impacted their lives forever. They were the ones who had stayed sleepless overnight, working tirelessly, yet catching nothing. And now, in the most unfavourable fishing conditions, they have filled up two boatloads. Simon received blessings from the Lord, through God's generous grace and favour.

Simon realised Jesus was not just a street preacher, a handyman carpenter, or someone to rub salt into his wounded pride because of an unsuccessful fishing activity. Maybe he debated in his mind, 'If Jesus can direct me to fill two boats full of fish, then... He is someone more than what we perceived Him to be!'

His first reaction after the miracle had sunk in was to approach the Rabbi with a repentant heart. *"Depart from me, for I am a sinful man, O Lord!"*

But with a loving and assuring voice, Jesus called all four of them out to their new career. *"Do not be afraid. From now on you will catch men (fishers of men)."*

Later, Jesus foresaw Simon's role in the Church and gave him the title, Peter (John 1:42, Matt 16:13-20), or Cephas in Aramaic, Kepha in Hebrew, and Petros in Greek. The name Peter was given to Simon as a title and not a proper name, in a way like Jesus has the title Christ, the Anointed One. Jesus also gave the brothers, James and

John, sons of Zebedee, the title *Boanerges*, the 'Sons of Thunder' alluding to their intense, outspoken personalities.[14]

Simon Confronted with Change

When a transformation happens, we undergo a Change Cycle[15] in our lives, and we see this in the life of Simon.

1. **The Current Scenario**

   Simon's daily business cycle was engaging in his commercial undertaking. Change starts where you are right now. The present state is where your story begins, where the Saviour meets you and initiates the journey. What is your current condition that has prompted you to consider a transformation?

2. **The Obstruction/Challenge**

   God allowed Simon and his mates to experience an unsuccessful business event to bring about a reason to change. There are times when, professionally, you realise the Lord is trying to get your attention by placing a wall in your area of specialisation. The very occupation you work at day in and day out, which has kept you and your family fed for years, is now tuning you out of the frequency of His Spirit. Are you facing a barrier in your business or career? Has the Lord initiated a situation to get your attention? God will meet you in your workplace.

3. **The Solution Proposal**

   Jesus proposed a fisheries solution for these professional fishermen. Neither the methodology nor the resolution itself were industry standard. But in God's kingdom, who do these results rely on?

---

[14] Mark 3:17 notes NKJV MacArthur Study Bible, 2nd Ed.
[15] The Change Cycle: https://changecycle.com/change-cycle

4. The Execution of the Solution

Peter went against his practical business sense and followed this carpenter's instruction. Was this his act of faith? Did he even know enough about this street preacher to respond in faith? Both the source and the solution to the obstacle were not logical *best practices*.

The outcome of the proposed solution is based on **who is the giver** of the resolution, which is predetermined by God's purpose and not how great the *faith* of the participant is, much less their expertise or the methodology of the solution.

5. The Invitation to Change

Peter was then invited to accept the change. Jesus called him to a career change from being a fisherman to a *fisher of men*. Because he witnessed this personal miracle, he accepted the invitation and followed Jesus. *"Follow Me, and I will make you fishers of men."* Matthew 4:19

Likewise, Jesus challenged Andrew, James, and John. And they all followed Him.

The Personality of Simon that Brought About Change

1. Available and Willing

It was a simple request from a Rabbi who was teaching His followers to borrow Simon's boat and use it as a platform so all could hear Him clearly. Imagine if Simon had declined the request. He would have missed that opportunity. However, Simon responded positively. The key was being *available* and *willing* to be a channel of blessing to others, allowing that opportunity to be blessed in return and receive a miracle.

2. **Anti-Change**

It is normal for humans to resist change. The instruction of Jesus may sound simple and straightforward, but like the disciples, we may also have these valid reasons to oppose the proposed action to transform:
- *Professional Advantage* – Simon's team were experienced fishermen. "We know better than you."
- *Physically Hammered* – The fishermen had toiled the whole night, tired, exhausted, and hungry. They believed they no longer had enough physical capability to undergo the change.
- *Psychologically Battered* – Mentally and emotionally tired after an unproductive night. Professionally, they all came from a failed undertaking, and their morale and confidence were low.
- *Phase of Acceptance* – Resigned to their unfavourable result, they had come to terms with their situation and had proceeded to the next phase of their business cycle: cleaning and mending their nets. They resisted the change because they were resolved to move on.

These feelings to resist change exist as a normal part of our humanity, and like hunger and tiredness, serve as building blocks for our faith to grow. These attitudes help us rely more on the God we believe in, beyond the weakness of our mortality.

3. **Accepting the Challenge to Change**

Beaten and battered in his pride, profession, and personality, Simon still knew his place, *"Master…, nevertheless at Your word, I will let down the net."* Even in Simon's qualified, mental and experiential objections, he obeyed the words of Jesus. When you accept Jesus as your Lord and Saviour, you must expect that there will be times when God's *"thoughts are not your thoughts,"* (Isaiah 55:8) and that the things He wants you to do can sometimes be illogical or against how you were trained as a skilled professional. That is why it is vital that you have a very close relationship with your Father and recognise His voice when He is telling you what you need to do.

At times, you will face a dead-end through the futility of your resistance to His instructions. You will end up struggling to move forward in areas you know you are good at. You must take this matter personally, as a special message directed only to you. You know deep down, and you must do it. Simon knew he needed to let down his nets because this Rabbi said so.

4. Appreciating the Catch

Look for the miracles that are happening in your life. We often overlook the miracles and blessings of everyday life, like perfect weather on the beach, or the veggie patch producing nice leafy greens for your sandwich. But like Simon and his team, you must be mindful and appreciate the miracles happening in your workplace that people would often label as coincidence, luck, or just plain genius of the team to get the thing working successfully. Appreciate the miracles!

5. Authentic Self-Evaluation

Simon's attitude toward the bountiful catch is worth noting. He didn't celebrate the abundance as if he had just won the lottery, but instead went straight to the source of the miracle. When prosperity and plenty come, for some, this means a prospective luxurious lifestyle. For these fishermen this catch meant something different. Abundance did not get into the head of Simon and draw him away from Jesus. On the contrary, it led him nearer to Him with a repenting heart. *"Depart from me, for I am a sinful man, O Lord!"*

6. Apprehensiveness

Like *Anti Change*, Fear is another typical reaction to an overwhelming situation. Fear is the first natural emotional response when men are confronted by the glory of the Lord and realise how sinful they are. But here, Jesus encouraged Simon not to be anxious with a comforting and assuring statement, *"Do not be afraid."*

> ### Bible Fact!
>
> *'Do not be afraid'* or *'Fear not'* is written 365 times in the Bible! Rick Warren said,
>
> *"It's interesting to note that there are 365 verses in the Bible that say, 'Fear not.' God provided us with one 'Fear not' message for every day of the year! He wants us to hear the message: Don't be afraid.*
>
> *"Why does God have to repeat himself so often when it comes to our worries and fears? It's because our hurts and hang-ups can often cause us to think that God is out to get us, that all he wants to do is condemn us and punish us. But that simply isn't true. Jesus is the proof of that."* [1]
>
> It is thought-provoking that almost every time God talks to someone in the Bible, He first says, *"Don't be afraid!"*

You must hold on to this assuring advice, for this will carry you through the challenges of the new career.

In this time of change, here are the prominent reasons why fear is prevalent in the area of profession or career:

   a. **Fear of uncertainty** – You have lived in the comfort of certainty and established your career, job or business, day in and day out. Having things predictable is tantamount

to being in control, and a new and unfamiliar career increases one's fear.
   b. **Fear of financial insecurity** – When inflation (as in 2022) shoots up prices and the cost of living, a fixed income or salary gives us a good sense of security. Having a family to support, kids in school and maybe a mortgage to pay, keeps people in their comfort zone of financial security. One of the significant factors to consider when changing careers, if not the major one, is the remuneration the new job will provide.
   c. **Fear of lost relationships** – Moving to a new country, city, job, or school requires one to detach from existing relationships and start anew. For most, this is a very stressful situation as some former relationships may have been their support groups and emotional anchors.
   d. **Fear of being inadequate** – Relearning a new skill is sustainable if all the supports are in place. Working in a new, more challenging role than the previous one, can lead to a sense of insufficiency of skills and experience. A designated role or position can come with high performance expectations from the organisation. To take this giant leap, some will require reasonable time and training to fit into the new role during the transition period.

7. **Absolute Commitment**

"... they forsook all and followed Him." Luke 5:11 The mission Jesus had for these *fishers of men* required complete dedication and commitment. They needed to see this miraculous catch to be willing to give up everything. Turning their backs on an existing career or occupation was not easy. They were leaving behind all the time and money invested in building their trade or business. This investment had been made to gain respect, experience, and a name within this secured profession. But the specific call to these first disciples required them to give up those investments and achievements to follow Jesus. They were waiting for the Messiah, as all Jews were. These fishermen *knew* Jesus was indeed the Messiah the moment they pulled up their nets. The

disciples believed they were leaving their craft to serve the promised King, as foretold in the Scriptures. They acted according to their faith and what it required.

Pause for Thought

Change does not come easily, nor does it come without obstacles or fears. We can plan on paper way ahead of time when we will change course in our lives. For example, graduating at age 20, working ten years in a prestigious company, aspiring to be a manager for five years, get to the executive level, be a CEO of an influential online company at 45, and maybe retire at 50. This is a good plan. However,

> *"A man's heart plans his way, But the Lord directs his steps."* Proverbs 16:9

> *"There are many plans in a man's heart, Nevertheless the Lord's counsel—that will stand."* Proverbs 19:21

Our Heavenly Father directs the changes we need in our lives, and He will definitely get our attention so they come to pass. And it is our responsibility to respond.

Prayer Point

*Dear Heavenly Father,
I pray for my brothers and sisters in the family of Christ, that You speak to their hearts and make it clear in their lives and spirits what Your plans are for them.
I also intercede for those whom You are calling now to change.
Yes, there are obstacles in their path,
but please remove them and make Your way plain to them.
In Jesus' name, Amen*

"Do you love Me?"

Let us fast forward to the time *after* the resurrection of Jesus in John 21:

"I am going fishing," Peter said to the six disciples around him. This was after witnessing the resurrection of their Master, and twice seeing the appearance of Jesus personally. In addition, he carried the burden of rejecting the Teacher he loved, not once, not twice, but three times, even after boasting he would defend Jesus to the death. To be around Jesus, listening to His teachings, following Him for three revealing years of His public ministry, and then suddenly, for Him to no longer be with them must have shaken their faith. They were like an army without a leader; directionless, aimless, and alone.

"We are going with you also." The rest of the disciples decided to return to their old commercial fishing trade.

Retreating back to our comfort zone is the most logical and practical step to feel as though we are achieving again when change *seems* to bring failure. When larger-than-life obstacles appear to stand in the way of God's calling, when resources dwindle and bills inflate, faith begins to stretch like a thin elastic band, and you fear that your situation will pull it far enough to snap!

In his sermon, **"Peter, do you love me?",** Pastor John MacArthur explains the scene in John 21: *"I told you, they were supposed to be on a mountain waiting for the Lord, but Peter decided that he was going to abandon his call to ministry, if you will, and go back to fishing. There were reasons for that. He had denied the Lord on three separate occasions. I think he felt inadequate. I think he felt guilty. I think he felt weak. He also was a man who didn't have a lot of patience. He had not yet, along with the apostles, received the Holy Spirit. They were doubtful of their own power, their own ability, to sustain a ministry he knew that he had failed so many times."*[16]

---

[16] **Peter, Do You Love Me?** John MacArthur, November 20, 2016: https://www.gty.org/library/sermons-library/43-116/peter-do-you-love-me

The night was quiet and still, a favourable condition for a good catch. The moonlight reflected smoothly on the calm water as they waited. They drew up their nets to check, as no activity had been observed below since they had lowered their nets. There was nothing. However, their persistence in searching for meaning and fulfilment, made them go through the cycle repeatedly; yet the entire night ended as in a fruitless endeavour. Their enthusiasm at the beginning of the night now turned into dejection, despair and gloom.

When their sore arms pulled up the nets one last time, maybe they heard a rooster crow faintly in the distance, a sign the dawn was about to break. Slowly, the early morning started to paint the sky deep red. The dreary eyes of the fishermen stared at the horizon as the sun began to rise to its fullness, shining on their weary, oily faces. They were about to end their trawling pursuit unproductively.

Then they heard someone calling from the shore, *"Children, do you have any fish?"*

"No." they replied.

"Cast the net on the right side of the boat, and you will find some." Not knowing it was Jesus, they blindly followed the stranger's suggestion. They shifted their net to the right side of the boat and apathetically dropped it down again into the Sea of Tiberias.

Behold, their sore muscles started to contract due to the weight of the heavy net! They could not haul it in, for the net was full; one hundred and fifty-three fish were caught. Then they remembered.

"It is the Lord!" John shouted, pointing in the direction of the voice. It was indeed the Lord again meeting them in the most vulnerable situation of their profession. Peter eagerly jumped off the boat, still 100 metres away from the shore (the second time Simon got off a boat to meet Jesus!). His purpose for being, he now saw in this Person. He was like a long-lost orphan who finds his father.

Instead of being reprimanded because they had abandoned their calling, these weary disciples were greeted with the aroma of freshly baked, coal-fired bread, and grilled fish. Jesus invited them to also bring some of the fish they had just miraculously caught to the fire. Jesus fed and met the needs of these physically tired, emotionally bruised and battered men who had faithfully followed Him, experienced His ministry, and witnessed His death and resurrection.

Jesus knows our needs. Just as He knew the immediate needs of His beloved disciples, and He met those needs, and healed and restored them.

This miracle the disciples received wasn't only the 153 fish, but in that gift of abundance, their nets did not break! The actual abundance the Lord gives is safe, and this abundance will not 'break' what having plenty usually breaks: family, relationships, attitudes, character, etc. God supports, God blesses, and God gives to overflowing.

After Jesus met the immediate physical needs of His seven disciples, He started to address the elephant in the room, so to speak, and tie up the loose ends that Peter and the others had concerning their calling, that had driven them back to being fishermen.

"Do you love me?" Jesus asked as He looked with compassionate eyes at Simon Peter. In this face-to-face dialogue, Jesus aimed to remove the haze of Peter's perception of himself and his commitment to his Master, reaffirming what was in his heart and mind and who he could become.

Why do you think Jesus asked Peter this question three times? As a teenager and a young Christian, I simulated the situation; what if my Lord asked me the same question, *"Do you love me?"* three times? I turned to the original Greek text of this event and focused squarely on the original word of the question… "love". This is how the conversation impressed me. For the first two questions, He used the Greek word, Agape (ἀγαπᾷς με), the purest form of love, God's love, and Simon responded with Phileo – brotherly or relational love (φιλῶ σε). The third time Jesus asked Simon, He used Phileo (φιλεῖς με). Being asked for the third time, Simon was then saddened and responded that he loved (φιλῶ σε) Jesus. Saddened, because I believe Jesus asked Simon about a lower type of love the third time.

After this discourse, Jesus commissioned Simon to *"Feed His lambs… tend His sheep… and feed His sheep."* The same as when Jesus first called the fishermen to become fishers of men (Matthew 4:19), Jesus said to him, *"Follow Me."* This was a full circle to complete Peter's change cycle.

How do you deal with the hard questions our Lord asks you in your new career?

Distractions: Yes, there will be distractions throughout your journey. Simon's distraction at this time was John.

"But Lord, what about *this* man?"

Jesus' perfect and straightforward response was, *"If I will that he remain till I come, what is that to you?"*

But instead, He reminded Peter what he really needed to keep his mind on, ***"You follow Me."***

Our Lord found the disciples back in their comfort zone. There, He reached out, refreshed them physically, restored them, re-established their faith and revived them with a new miracle. He will address the questions that matter most to you and the issues that are keeping you from moving forward.

Here is a high-level profile of Simon's life in the Gospels.

Timeframe	Scenario
Life before Jesus	Simon was a fisherman
	Simon's brother was Andrew
	Simon was married
	Brothers James and John were his fishing mates
	Lived in Capernaum
Trigger: Jesus asked Simon to cast his net and he encountered the miraculous catch - Luke 5:1-11	
Life during the ministry of Jesus	Followed Jesus with his brother Andrew and their friends James and John along with eight other men as disciples
	Learned and witnessed the life and works of Jesus the promised Messiah
	Was named Simon Peter
	Witnessed the death and resurrection of Jesus
Trigger: Jesus asked the disciples, who were fishing again, to cast their nets for another miraculous catch - John 21	
Life after the ascension of Jesus	Peter led the selection of Matthias to replace Judas among the 11 apostles - Acts 1:16-26
	Peter was filled with the power of the Holy Spirit at Pentecost -Acts 2:14-36
	Peter proclaimed the Good News to the Jews and to the Gentiles
	Peter was crucified in AD64 as a martyr for Jesus

Section Summary

When you are called out of your comfort zone and into a life of faith, an environment or career where you have little or no experience, it is a very uncomfortable but worthwhile journey. However, when challenges come, and the bumps on the road seem to grow out of proportion, you may tend to look back to the comfortable couch you used to enjoy.

Your faith is undergoing a situation well-identified in the *Elastic Band illustration*. When you take that first step of faith, your life feels like an elastic band, and it is certain that your faith will be stretched during this journey. There will come a point where you will feel your band is being overextended, and you start to sense your faith is about to fracture. Our Heavenly Father knows what you are going through. He knows your every need and worry. He will meet you there, and He promises He will meet your needs.

Section Questions

1. Are you currently facing an obstacle or a *wall* in your business or career? Is this obstacle making you evaluate your present career? Do you consider this your 'empty net' experience?

2. Do you think God is using this obstacle to get your attention?

3. Have you encountered a professional or business drought?

4. Has professional or business abundance or success hindered your service to God?

5. Has the Holy Spirit been trying to get your attention in the past or recently?

6. How have you let the Lord use your business, talent, or profession to bless others? Or did you decline that opportunity?

7. What would your fears be if you were asked to change your career now? Write down your worries about a career or business change. What are you afraid of?

8. What do you think is the purpose of the miracle of the big catch to the fishermen?

9. Is God giving you an instruction that is professionally illogical or even not *best practice*?

10. How would you deal with any hard questions if our Lord asked you to go to this new career?

Additional Resource to the Character Profile of Simon Peter

The series, <u>The Chosen, Episode 4 of Season One,</u> portrayed this event in Luke 5:1-11 (Matt 4:18-22, Mark 1:16-20). Consolidate this chapter by viewing the video and reading the passages to bring meaning to the events in the life of Peter.

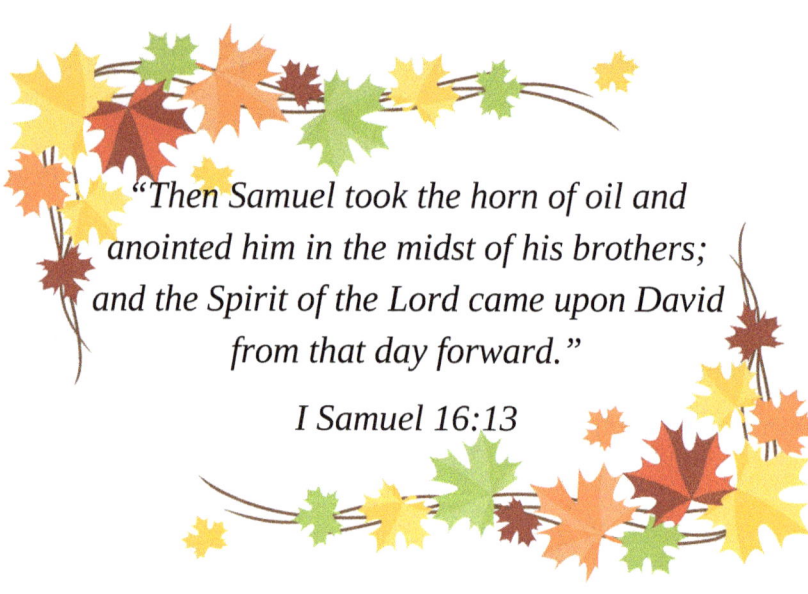

"Then Samuel took the horn of oil and anointed him in the midst of his brothers; and the Spirit of the Lord came upon David from that day forward."

I Samuel 16:13

Chosen and Consecrated

God's Career Development Plan

I SAMUEL 16:1-13

ONE OF THE WORLD'S MOST FAMOUS statues is Michelangelo's masterpiece, David. The original work by this master stands in a gallery in Florence, Italy. There are several replicas of this great work, from a life-size piece to a bust sculpture—all in tribute to a genius who has visually rendered a famous king. This inanimate object itself has several interesting stories that may match the person it portrays.

Michelangelo's David at its home in the Galleria dell'Accademia in Florence (Bevacqua, 2023)

Context is a travel website which lists Ten Facts about Michelangelo's Statue of David in Florence, Italy. [17] Here is the list:

1. The Statue of David is roughly the size of a two-storey building or an adult giraffe.
2. There are 30 life-sized replicas of David around the world.
3. David pre-dates Michelangelo: it was merely a rough slab of marble for ~35 years, deemed unusable for a sculpture until Michelangelo worked his magic.
4. The statue is disproportionate because of the marble block, which was previously deemed unworkable.
5. Michelangelo chose to break tradition with David, creating the statue without the head of Goliath.
6. The Statue of David is slightly cross-eyed – maybe intentionally.
7. It took four days and 40 men to move the Statue of David half a mile from Michelangelo's workshop to the Piazza.
8. Although beloved by Florentines, the Statue of David has been damaged several times outdoors.
9. David isn't perfectly protected indoors either – ask his left foot.
10. The Statue of David embodies the city of Florence, symbolizing independence and strength in the perfect image of youthful beauty.

Fact No. 3 is a very interesting story. This solid marble block took approximately 35 long years before it became the finely sculpted figure of the young future king of Israel; longer than it took to chisel out the leader from a teenage sheep herder, becoming the forefather of the Messiah.

The Statue of David was originally commissioned in 1464 by the Opera del Duomo, as part of a series of large statues for the Florence Cathedral. These were meant to be sculpted on the ground, then raised roughly 260 feet into the niches of the cathedral's tribunes.

The project was initially awarded to Agostino di Duccio, despite his lack of experience with large-scale sculpture. Duccio travelled

---

[17] https://www.contexttravel.com/blog/articles/ten-facts-about-the-statue-of-david

to the nearby quarries of Carrara to select a marble block, but his inexperience led him astray: he hewed a tall but narrow block full of imperfections, tiny holes, and visible veins. The quarry struggled to prepare and ship the massive block, and when it finally arrived in Florence, Duccio realized his error and gave up on the project. The block was untouched for 10 years until Antonio Rossellino tried to salvage the piece. He, too, quickly deemed the marble unusable, and the block lay in the courtyard of the Opera del Duomo for another 25 years.

Fact No. 4 perfectly illustrates what David experienced as a teenager before he was anointed to be the future king. He was overlooked! Even by his own dad.

Our character in this study did not experience a dramatic divine intervention, similar to that of Moses or Peter, to convince him of a career change. In fact, it took him 15 years from his first anointing to be crowned King of Judah and another three years before King David unified the Jewish kingdoms of Judah and Israel. In that process, David underwent three anointings before finally becoming king.

David was a very significant king in the history of Israel. He became the point of reference for the prophecy of the coming Messiah, and that Jesus would come from this Davidic line.

As the anointed future king of Israel, David's very own father overlooked him. Man's opinion and perception does not determine or undermine God's eternal plan and purpose. His career path had an extended *Career Development Plan* and experience before assuming the office of King. Likewise, the *Psalms of David* documented in poetic literature his mental state as he underwent all these events in his life.

An Overview of David's life:

Age	Period	Passage	Scenario
0-15	Shepherd's Life	I Samuel 16	Youngest son of eight by Jesse.
			Shepherd's skillset and profession
			Artist: Musician and Poet
			David was glowing with health, fine appearance and handsome
Trigger: Samuel anointed David to be the next king of Israel because God had rejected Saul			
15-30	Life to the throne	I Samuel 16 - 31	Continued to be a shepherd in his family
			Became an aide to the king's court
			Killed Goliath and became a popular warrior
			Became an outlaw and went into hiding across different countries due to the jealousy of King Saul who wanted him killed.
			David and Jonathan became good friends despite Jonathan being the king's son
			David took Abigail as his wife
			David had two opportunities to kill King Saul but spared his life
			Jonathan died in a battle and Saul took his own life
David anointed as King of Judah			
30-33	Reunification of Israel	II Samuel 2-5	War between the house of David and the house of Saul
			David's kingdom grew stronger and stronger
			David killed all his enemies
			David conquered Jerusalem
David anointed as King of Israel - II Samuel 5			

Overlooked

Have you ever experienced being overlooked, unnoticed by your manager, or being left out of the recent run of promotions in the office? Was your resume chucked under the pile in your current application for a job opportunity?

I was looking for my next employment with an application for a technical position through a recruitment company. However, I was rejected for the position. The candidate manager told me the reason for not getting the role was that my skill set was overtly attuned to one major brand of technology which did not suit the tasks in this role. Getting rejected was hard enough, but being overlooked was yet another psychological struggle to deal with.

The Lord Yahweh told the Prophet Shmu-el (Hebrew pronunciation of Samuel) to fill his horn with oil in preparation to anoint a new king to replace Saul, who had outrightly disobeyed His command to utterly exterminate the Amalekites and their assets. God specifically told Shmu-el to go to Jesse the Bethlehemite's house, for in that family the Lord would show him who would be the future king. The Lord told Shmu-el to take a heifer and use the occasion of sacrificing to Yahweh as an excuse to meet with the family of Jesse to avoid raising any suspicion from Saul regarding this event. The invitation by Shmu-el surprised and worried Jesse, especially when the prophet requested his entire household to be present on this unexpected visit to his town. But Shmu-el appeased Jesse's fear which was understandable.

Predictably, David, still a teenager and the youngest in Jesse's family of eight sons, was faithfully tending his father's sheep. He could have noticed that day something was different.

'Hey', he may have thought, 'where are my brothers? Leaving me all alone again with Dad's flocks!' As a fifteen-year-old herdsman, he knew his job well. He had tended his father's sheep with exceptional skill and an acute sense of responsibility. He had also developed and harnessed his warrior-skills by protecting the sheep from poachers and predators. Later, he highlighted his competence when Saul questioned his abilities, measuring his tender age against Goliath's years of experience:

"Your servant has been keeping his father's sheep. When a lion or a bear came and carried off a sheep from the flock, I went after it, struck it and rescued the sheep from its mouth. When it turned on

me, I seized it by its hair, struck it and killed it. Your servant has killed both the lion and the bear; this uncircumcised Philistine will be like one of them, because he has defied the armies of the living God. **<u>The Lord</u>** <u>*who rescued me from the paw of the lion and the paw of the bear will rescue me from the hand of this Philistine.*</u>" 1 Samuel 17:34-37

What faith!

In worship, declare this statement:

"The Lord who has watched over me and provided faithfully all these years, WILL …_____" AMEN!

But on this occasion, David was overlooked by Jesse, his own father! Shmu-el started with the eldest, Eliab, the most obvious candidate to be the next King of Israel. By description, he possessed a kingly external stature, posture, and strength, but these were not what the Lord wanted in the king who would represent Him and lead His people. One by one, Shmu-el had all of David's seven older brothers pass by him, yet Yahweh did not show His approval to any of them. When the last one had passed in front of him, Shmu-el became perplexed. *"Are all the young men here?"* he asked.

While men may overlook, the Lord sees and has complete knowledge of the specific individual for His divine plan. Even when you are busy at work with your regular daily business activities, and nothing makes you stand out on the factory floor, God knows you by name and will pick you out from the crowd to accomplish His will.

Jesse replied, *"There remains yet the youngest, and there he is, keeping the sheep."*

"Send and bring him. For we will not sit down till he comes here," Shmu-el adamantly insisted.

Imagine being in David's sandals watching over the flock on a bright sunny day, living a shepherd's life. Perhaps he had just finished herding the sheep for a drink from *'still waters'* and was now under a shady tree. While relaxing, he may have taken his harp and started singing a Psalm he had written, while his sheep lay *'down in green pastures.'*

"David! David! You must come now! Dad is calling for you."

"But, but what about the sheep? Who is going to look after them?"

David was then abruptly pulled away from his duty at his workplace. Unprepared, this *'ruddy, bright-eyed, good-looking'* and sheep-smelling, 15-year-old lad was suddenly pushed in front of a prominent figure, Shmu-el. *"Arise, anoint him; for this is the one!"* the Lord said. Then Shmu-el took the horn of oil and anointed him in the midst of his brothers..."

'What is this happening to me? Why am I being smothered by this oil!' David might have said in his mind as Shmu-el firmly gripped this young man's shoulder and tipped the horn over, drizzling the oil onto the teenager's curly hair. *"...and the Spirit of the Lord came upon David <u>from that day forward</u>."* David was anointed to a new career path, to the throne of Israel, which would take a further **15 years**!

Be strong and courageous! Our Heavenly Father has not and will not overlook you. In their limited capacity and knowledge, men rely only on what they can perceive. They base their decisions on what is written in a person's resume or reference given by a referee. But the Lord knows you inside-out and has specifically chosen you.

"For the Lord does not see as man sees; for man looks at the outward appearance, but the Lord looks at the heart." I Samuel 16:7b

Career Development Plan

Back in high school, my future career was one of the most overwhelming, if not the *only* thing running through this teenager's fragile and developing mind! What course should I take at the university? There were factors that put pressure on me: Firstly, this crucial decision would ultimately seal my destiny. What did I want to be? Secondly, I didn't want to waste four years of my youth ending up moving to another field of work. I wanted to maximise my learning, and make the best use of my time for the vocation I wanted to engage in for the rest of my life. Thirdly, though I was enrolled at a state university, the University of the Philippines, where tuition was subsidised, we would still need to fork out a significant amount to complete a degree. I asked the Lord to lead me to the course He wanted me to take for the next four years.

The door opened for me to take a degree in electrical engineering, which was also one of my interests. To make the long story short, God's educational program for me was not clear at the start.

After various circumstances and struggles, I finally graduated with a Communications Major. Well, there went my career planning. But God knew best what I needed to move forward.

Aside from investing time and resources towards a degree, I later pursued a career as an application and technical trainer in the digital field. In this business, I needed to keep myself upskilled, learning new versions and products that software companies occasionally released. This also updated my professional certification as a trainer and technology specialist. This was part of my Continuing Professional Development (CPD).

At fifteen, David's career was predetermined when he was chosen by Yahweh, who instructed Shmu-el to set him apart from his brothers and anoint him as the future king of Israel. His Continuing Professional Development to be king was a fifteen-year-long learning process. This was not all done in the halls of the palace of King Saul with all his advisers and generals and a fixed curriculum on how to lead a nation and a kingdom. Instead, David continued to shepherd Jesse's flock, until he fought and killed a Philistine giant who insulted his countrymen and, more importantly, his God.

Then came his time of running and hiding as a fugitive because the incumbent King of Israel, Saul, had become angry and jealous of him. However, in the middle of all these tense events was the assurance that the Spirit of the Lord was with David.

This was the critical phase in the calling of David, when *"the Spirit of the Lord came upon"* him. This was "an external symbol of an inward work of God. The operation of the Holy Spirit, in this case, was not just for regeneration but for empowerment to perform his (David's) role in God's program for Israel (cf. Saul, 1 Sam. 10:6). After David sinned with Bathsheba (2 Sam. 11, 12), he prayed, *"...Do not take Your Holy Spirit from me"* (Ps. 51:11)[18]. The anointment made him conscious of this process, its path and destination, just like enrolling in a university. He also accepted that this journey would take him on to be the King of Israel. In the early part of his relationship with King Saul, he was called to the king's presence when the *"Spirit of the Lord departed from Saul and a distressing spirit from the Lord troubled him."* 1 Samuel 16:14. His pleasant manner with the king led him to become one of his armourbearers. And his skilful music would *"refresh and make Saul feel better."* He also went to the front lines as a true warrior for the king.

What a career path for a future king! This type of career change requires endurance. Have you encountered that *anointment* milestone in your life? This would be an important event in your life where God has talked to you in either a gentle but convincing voice or an earth-shaking wake-up call. This gives you the battle cry to help you get through the months or years of both good and bad days; times when you feel God is right beside you, or you might have been tempted to think He has left you alone.

You should be blessed (anointed) with a passage from His Word, a promise, or an instruction that you can write in your spiritual diary and on the tablet of your heart (to memorise). Some call this *life verse*, but this is YOUR instruction from the Lord. This personal note from God is between you and Him, and not from some spiritual authority telling you specifically what to do. Spend time in your *closet* (prayer room, or War Room – an Alex Kendrick movie) with the Lord, giving Him time to reveal His Word to you. Or, just like David, God can pick you out from where you are to have a personal

---

[18] The MacArthur Study Bible, Word Publishing, 1997.

encounter with Jesus. The Word of our Lord is your *anchor* in times of storm, your Polaris (North Star), that keeps your course straight and sure regardless of any circumstances.

> *"But this is the covenant that I will make with the house of Israel after those days, says the Lord: I will put My law in their minds, and write it on their hearts; and I will be their God, and they shall be My people."* Jeremiah 31:33

> *"I delight to do Your will, O my God, And Your law is within my heart."* Psalm 40:8

The Mind of David

The Scriptures have devotedly documented the lives of men and women in their walk of faith with their Heavenly Father. The authors wrote these accounts to inspire generations of believers, strengthen their faith, and their belief in the righteous character of our Lord. But we shouldn't stop asking ourselves what was in the minds of these giants when they faced the imminent dangers of death, the prolonged pursuit of the enemy, the discouragements of life, and their struggles with sin and temptation. These are things we can easily relate to when we are in the dark spaces of our lives.

David wrote many of the Psalms. Scholars believe he wrote at least 73 of the 150 (some attribute two more for a total of 75). In these Psalms, David described what he was thinking and feeling while undergoing these difficult circumstances. This is an excellent opportunity to view and study the mental well-being or headspace of someone God called, '… *a man after My own heart…*'.

From a shepherd's point of view, let us revisit one of the most quoted and loved Psalms of David:

Psalm 23

A Psalm of David.

The Lord is my shepherd;
I shall not want.
He makes me to lie down in green pastures;
He leads me beside the still waters.
He restores my soul;
He leads me in the paths of righteousness
For His name's sake.

Yea, though I walk through the valley of the shadow of death,
I will fear no evil;
For You are with me;
Your rod and Your staff, they comfort me.

You prepare a table before me in the presence of my enemies;
You anoint my head with oil;
My cup runs over.
Surely goodness and mercy shall follow me
All the days of my life;
And I will dwell in the house of the Lord
Forever.

As I meditated on this Psalm, it revealed to me the heart of our Heavenly Father and how He loves us and watches over us. But I must also consider that this wonderful Psalm, though it was truly beautifully written, is subject to the limitation of human perspective, experience and language while trying to comprehend an infinite God.

> **Point for Worship**
> *Pause for a moment,
> and worship our Heavenly Shepherd.*
>
> *~*
>
> *Meditate in worship with this song by Chris Tomlin,
> 'Goodness, Love and Mercy' – his version of Psalm 23.
> I hope this will bless your heart as it did mine.*

Here are two of snippets of David's Psalms during his 15 years of continuing professional development:

Psalm 56

When the Philistines had seized David in Gath.

> *Be merciful to me, my God,
> for my enemies are in hot pursuit;
> all day long they press their attack.
> My adversaries pursue me all day long;
> in their pride many are attacking me.*
>
> *When I am afraid, I put my trust in you.
> In God, whose word I praise—
> in God I trust and am not afraid.
> What can mere mortals do to me?*

Psalm 57

When David had fled from Saul into the cave

> *I am in the midst of lions;
> I am forced to dwell among ravenous beasts—
> men whose teeth are spears and arrows,
> whose tongues are sharp swords.*
>
> *Be exalted, O God, above the heavens;
> let your glory be over all the earth.*

David showed how human and vulnerable he could be in his writings, yet the Spirit of the Lord was with him, and at the end of his discourse, he raised his voice and body in praise and worship to God for His greatness, goodness, and love.

Narrative Digest

> *"Your eyes saw my substance,*
> *being yet unformed.*
> *And in Your book they all were written,*
> *The days fashioned for me,*
> *When as yet there were none of them."*
>
> Psalm 139:16

Psalm 139 of David proclaims our Lord's sovereignty over his life. Unlike Moses or Peter, a third-party entity – the prophet Shmuel – ordained the direction of his future career. At 15, David was anointed to be the future king of Israel. God placed David for the next fifteen years in His divine Career Development Plan to produce the king after God's own heart.

The Lord could have called you or anointed you to a profession or career to serve His purpose at a certain point in your life, but the commissioning or the realisation of this calling could take years or even decades. Like David, your training period is all within the Lord's timetable, based on the curriculum He has set for each of His children. From the Psalms David wrote, we can all empathise with him, that life during this phase was hard and emotionally draining. But God knows how to shape your personality and capabilities, just as Michelangelo chiselled that imperfect block of marble into an enduring and priceless monument to a great king.

Likewise, David lifted his heart and his hands to the Almighty, who had full control over his life. We should continually learn from David how to worship and praise Yahweh for His love and grace in our lives regardless of the circumstances we are undergoing. Lift your voice of praise and declaration to our Lord!

Section Questions:

1. How does it feel to be overlooked or dismissed as a candidate for a position, a project, a job, a role, a promotion, a leadership activity, or a partner in a venture?

2. If you could foresee the ups and downs of your career, would you still stick to the existing job or choose another that looks easier?

3. Reading how David replied to King Saul in I Samuel 17:34-37, how do you think David could confidently make that statement?

4. David was anointed to this new career path. Have you experienced this anointing in your life and feel that the Lord's Spirit is with you?

5. Are you in a long-term career program, and is this career path giving you a clearer picture of what the Lord wants you to achieve? Or do you feel you need more support on this journey?

6. Was being the King of Israel a secular or spiritual vocation?

7. When you are offered a new job, either internally or externally, do you pause and think about how this fits in God's greater plan for your professional life?

8. Do you have that dedicated time to be with God, or a place you call your prayer closet (an isolated and undisturbed time and place with your Lord)? If not, set one. Make it a recurring meeting. Set it now.

9. Examine your professional/business skills now. Do you see how God's purpose fits those skills?

10. Reading and understanding what is in David's mind amid the tensions in his life, how has this perspective helped you with your faith in our Lord?

Additional Character Resources

1. War Room – an Alex Kendrick Movie

2. The David Movie – An animated movie project

3. Goodness, Love and Mercy – Psalm 23, performed by Chris Tomlin

4. More articles with facts about the Statue of David by Michelangelo:

    a. https://www.thecollector.com/10-facts-about-michelangelo-david-sculpture/

    b. https://www.accademia.org/explore-museum/artworks/michelangelos-david/facts-about-david/

    c. https://theflorenceinsider.com/fun-facts-michelangelo-david/

    d. https://www.michelangelo.org/david.jsp

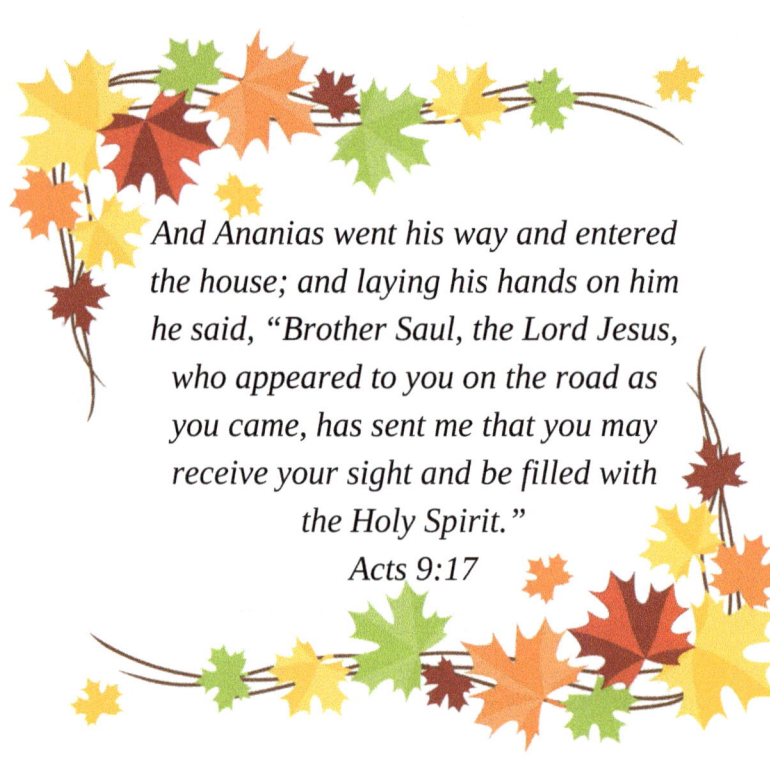

And Ananias went his way and entered the house; and laying his hands on him he said, "Brother Saul, the Lord Jesus, who appeared to you on the road as you came, has sent me that you may receive your sight and be filled with the Holy Spirit."
Acts 9:17

Vocational Epiphany

From A Promising Career

Paul's Testimonies

Acts 9:1-31
Acts 22
Acts 26:1-23

A Man Named Saul

Saul was born in Tarsus in the province of Cilicia, grew up in Jerusalem, and was a member of the tribe of Benjamin. As a Jew, he had the privilege of becoming a Pharisee. As a Roman citizen, he was also privileged to learn the knowledge of the Greeks.

John MacArthur has an excellent introduction to this man, *"In keeping with the Jewish tradition, every young boy had to learn a trade, and young Saul was taught to weave cloth out of black goat's hair and fashion it into strips that could be assembled together, sewn together, to make tents. This was a common industry in Tarsus.*

At about 13, when a Jewish boy would become officially a son of the law, it is very likely that at that time, Saul was packed off to Jerusalem. Why did he go there? Because his family wanted him to study Judaism at the highest level, and the highest level was to study under a teacher named Gamaliel. This man was so elevated and so revered as a teacher that he himself was called the beauty of the law. That was to say that the law was never more beautiful than when it was articulated by Gamaliel.

So, Saul would sit under the teaching of Gamaliel. This would include years of memorizing the Old Testament, years of intense question and answer, arguing and debating back-and-forth on the law of the Old Testament. He would become expert in Judaism, expert in the Old Testament."[19]

Saul had a very promising career in the Jewish community.

Jesus instigated the change. Here we will see, first, the dramatic encounter that started the change process in Paul's career; second, how he went through this massive change from a promising career; and third, the miraculous process he underwent for this change.

Blinded by Grace

Saul's radical change in the pursuit of his life goal was so distinct he changed from being a determined prosecutor of the perceived enemies of the Torah to a passionate evangelist for Jesus. It took an encounter with Jesus to bring this about.

At the end of chapter seven of the book of Acts, Doctor Luke wrote about the first incident where Paul is mentioned in Scripture, being described as *"a young man named Saul."* As a Pharisee, he witnessed with hearty approval, the execution of the first Christian martyr, Stephen. On that very day, great persecution began in Jerusalem against the church and the followers of Jesus Christ, and Saul was at the centre of this oppressive pursuit—going from house to house, hauling men and women away to prison. He went from city to city to arrest and persecute them, sincerely believing he was championing the cause of YHWH God. His zeal for the Law prompted him to lead the charge. This was Saul's purpose in life.

In Acts 22:3-5, Paul testified, *"I am indeed a Jew, born in Tarsus of Cilicia, but brought up in this city at the feet of Gamaliel, taught according to the strictness of our fathers' law, and was zealous toward God as you all are today. I persecuted this Way to the death, binding and delivering into prisons both men and women, as also the high priest bears me witness, and all the council of the elders, from whom I also received letters to the brethren, and went to*

---

[19] MacArthur, The Astounding Conversion of Paul, 2015

Damascus to bring in chains even those who were there to Jerusalem to be punished."

After Saul's encounter and conversation with Jesus on the road to Damascus, he became a committed advocate of the Christian faith and a faithful follower of Christ. From that point on, he travelled around most of the Mediterranean region, making three missionary journeys and planting at least five churches, Galatia, Philippi, Thessalonica, Corinth, and Ephesus. However, some scholars would attribute around fourteen during his time. Out of the 27 books of the New Testament, most scholars credit thirteen to him (seven are certain, and some dispute the other six).

Traditionally, the book of Hebrews was attributed to Paul, but it could also be by another early church leader such as Barnabas, Silas, Apollos, Luke, Philip, Priscilla, Aquila, or Clement of Rome, as the letter doesn't identify its writer. But no one can deny Paul's influence in the early stages of church history. By the Holy Spirit at Pentecost and through Paul's outreach, thousands came to the saving knowledge of Jesus. This became Paul's new purpose in life.

Career Disruption

Would you consider changing from your existing job, where you are suitably educated, trained, and equipped to a new career if a company offered you your dream role or job?

When you have the capital investment, market advantage, and a customer base all lined up for your business, would you consider changing your future endeavour?

What considerations or circumstances would make you leave a promising career or business?

Saul was privileged to gain an excellent education in both Judaism, under the tutelage of Gamaliel, and Greek, being a Roman citizen. Through these he had access to study Philosophy, Arts, Science, Law, and Religion. He was in a privileged position to grow his career and to have a bright future with a favourable career path.

As mentioned earlier, Saul was at the frontline of the Jewish faith in Acts 7, when Stephen was stoned to death—leading the way to protect the Torah and its institutions by stamping out the Hellenistic Jews (Jews living outside of Israel). They became believers in Jesus and were spreading the Good News of the risen Christ. He believed it was his duty and responsibility to stop this misinformation from spreading in the region.

Saul was an advocate of the Jewish religion and led the early believers' persecution. He initiated a *project* to help propagate and protect Judaism by going to the high priest and asking for letters of authority to take with him to Damascus, thereby sanctioning him to work on this project, which would also see his career star rise. Saul was on the edge of a promising career.

While Saul's future was soaring, God had other plans. When Saul's team were on their way to Damascus, at the brightest time of the day, a far more brilliant light suddenly astounded the project team.

"Saul, Saul, why do you persecute me?" An unfamiliar voice coming from the bright light resonated not only in Saul's ears but also targeted his heart, and he recognised he was in the presence of great authority.

"Who are you, Lord?"

"I am Jesus, whom you are persecuting."

Saul had a Divine Encounter with Jesus. The other members of the entourage also experienced the event but in a minimal capacity. They saw the bright light but didn't hear or understand the voice (Acts 22:9). Therefore, this was a precise personal encounter, as the Lord has shown in the past, He IS a personal God. This divinely instigated experience was directly meant for Saul.

Since Saul was a determined, dedicated Pharisee committed to their cause, the Lord Jesus—like a Zionist would confront a Roman soldier—opted to use this *road to Damascus* to engage with Saul and show him His plan. In this approach, it would be hard for Saul *"to kick against the goads."* (Acts 9:5, Acts 26:14) A goad was a stick used to poke and guide a stubborn animal in the direction the farmer wanted them to go. Through God's discretion, He knows the best way to communicate to you as His child through the Holy Spirit. He understands our limitations and our frailties. Therefore, He knows the best method to get His message through to you.

In May 2018, a group of dads and I started a local ministry for young boys aged 5-10. Initially, I had a burden for a Bible-based youth movement, like the Scouts, to teach life skills, discipline, and the love for Jesus, for I grew up in my younger years in a similar structure that helped me come to my Saviour, Jesus.

New Zealand has adapted the curriculum of a UK national programme called Boy's Brigade, to New Zealand settings, and called it ICONZ. The Lord pressed on my heart to start a unit in our local church when the Girls Brigade unit my daughter joined closed down, and one by one, other units in our suburb closed down too. Those units had difficulty finding people to pass the leadership onto. Our area now has less units to influence the younger generations with the message of Jesus. However, having only a burden for ministries is not enough; one must also commit to leading and maintaining them. God gave me a promise in His word from Psalm 112, verse two, *"Their children will be mighty in the land; the generation of the upright will be blessed."*

My journey didn't end there. I went to the head of the children's ministry in our local church and explained to her that God was calling me to start this ministry. After stubbornly delaying the inevitable by asking for more confirmation from God, she said, "I think you should talk to our pastor of community ministries."

Later, in my conversation with our pastor, she shared that just a month before this discussion, the development manager of BB/ICONZ NZ came knocking at the door of our church, introducing this ministry. Here, I could see the Lord was miraculously opening doors and creating opportunities to get this ministry started.

The next obstacle was having parent-leaders volunteer for the team, dads who would share their time with their own boys and others as Christian male models in their lives. Again, God provided, and four dads joined the team. These were the pieces of evidence I needed to commit my efforts to starting this ministry.

Then Covid-19 came, and ministries in my church went online during this period, or if that was not workable, stopped altogether. At this phase, all the original dads got busier or moved to different parts of the country. I prayed hard as I heard about the unavailability of each of the pioneers. "Is this the time to discontinue the ministry?" I asked the Lord.

And He said, "No! Just let them go." Then I asked God to provide more dads as we restarted this ministry, and He faithfully called them in. Do I need to be convinced? *"It is hard for you to kick against the goads."*

In God's foreknowledge of Saul, this experience was what he needed for his future ministry. God needed to recalibrate Saul's education, knowledge, and expertise towards the *Way* of our Lord Jesus Christ. This would redirect his strength, vision, and passion for proclaiming the Good News to the Gentiles, kings, and the Children of Israel. These were the changes required so Saul would be prepared for what the future held for him.

And later, Jesus selected and revealed to Ananias that he was to help the most feared person at that moment in history, for word had spread that Saul was sanctioning the imprisonment and killing of many believers. Ananias was to help Saul understand what was about to happen to him, *"For I will show him how many things he must suffer for My name's sake."* Acts 9:16

Saul forsook his promising career to gain his beloved Saviour, Jesus Christ!

Remember the movie *Chariots of Fire*? This is the true story of a Scottish Olympian named Eric Liddell. His story is famously known for his conviction not to run in his favourite event, the 100-metre race, as it was scheduled on a Sunday. He later won the gold medal in the 400-metre race. After the Olympics, when he was 23, he returned to China and served as a missionary. A video biography of Liddell entitled **The Story of Eric Liddell** – https://youtu.be/iAA8-13zQCg is a beautiful example of changing direction from a promising career.

Grace Unveiled: The Ananias Miracle

The miraculous transformation process of Saul happened on the road to Damascus, where Saul and his entourage were travelling the 218-kilometre journey from Jerusalem. Whenever they captured any followers of Jesus, they planned to take them to the Sanhedrin back in Jerusalem for trial. On this road came the initial miracle, a glaringly bright light, more brilliant than the sunniest time of day. The light was focused on Saul.

There came a voice from within that light, questioning the purpose of his mission. Then came the miraculous revelation of the identity of the voice. Saul did not know personally who Jesus was, nor did he witness Christ's life, ministry, judgement, and death. Saul only knew that Jesus had been a street preacher, that His teachings had agitated the teachers of the Torah, and now His followers were inexplicably growing exponentially, even though they had neither position nor authority in the synagogues. More importantly, the Judaic hierarchy had rejected Him as the promised Messiah. This Jesus of Nazareth was now in a deeply personal conversation with him through the voice within this astonishingly bright light. It was Jesus, and He was alive! As a result of this encounter, Saul was blinded (temporarily)! Therefore, he was dependent on the people in the team to get him to Damascus. Saul was visually impaired for three days. I believe God miraculously designed this, not to punish or contain him, but so he would have the time in solitude to reflect on what had just happened, and to fast and pray.

If you are in a debilitating situation, or in between jobs, made redundant, or just retired, take this *pause* moment to reflect on God's goodness and blessings, and fast and pray for God to reveal His glorious plan for your future.

Then came the Ananias miracle! Jesus revealed to Ananias in a vision about His encounter with Saul on the road, and explained the future for this man from Tarsus. Ananias did not know of Saul except that he had a reputation for violently persecuting followers of Jesus, arresting and taking them to Jerusalem, imprisoning them, and at times overseeing their execution. Saul was a feared person in the community of faith during that period. But Jesus explicitly told Ananias to meet with Saul, the persecutor of the believers.

Unbeknown to each other, these two men were to meet miraculously to execute a divine plan. Ananias went to the house of Judas in Straight Street, and there he found Saul helplessly blind, confused, and weak. He explained to Saul what Jesus had told him, how Saul had encountered Jesus on the way to Damascus, and how the event had unfolded. When Saul realised how precise the detailed account of the event was, he knew this was a miracle. Only Jesus could have told Ananias this, so Saul knew that He had assigned Ananias to minister to him. Ananias miraculously restored Saul's sight, filled him with the Holy Spirit, and baptised him in water. Saul ate and regained his strength. Ananias later introduced Saul to the other believers, and he spent several days with the disciples of Jesus in this miraculous fellowship.

"Let me tell you a guaranteed by-product of sincerely seeking His blessing: Your life will become marked by miracles."[20]

---

[20] B. Wilkinson, *The Prayer of Jabez*, ©2000, Multnomah Publishers, Inc.

Overview of Paul's Transformation

Age	Period	Passage	Scenario
0-33 Approx.	Life before Christ	Acts 7-9	Saul was born in Tarsus
			Saul was educated by the best of Jewish and Greek scholars
			Saul, as a Pharisee, witnessed and consented to the stoning of Stephen
			Saul was a Roman citizen
			Saul persecuted the early church of Jesus
			Plan to go to Damascus to persecute more Christians
Trigger: On his way to Damascus, Saul encountered Jesus with a bright light and was blinded after their conversation			
33-60 Approx	New life with Christ - 2 Corinthians 5:17, Galatians 2:20	Acts 9-28	Jesus called Ananias to meet, heal and baptise Saul in Damascus
			Saul met with Christ's disciples in Jerusalem
			Saul went to Arabia and learned directly from Jesus for 3 years. Galatians 1:12
			Saul started to preach about Jesus and people now wanted to kill him
			Barnabas brought Saul to Antioch
			"Then Saul, who also is called Paul…" Luke now started to refer to Saul as Paul in Acts 13:9
			Paul in Syria and Cilicia
			Paul's first missionary journey
			Paul explaining his mission in the Jerusalem Council
			Paul's second missionary journey
			Paul's third missionary journey
			Paul arrested in Jerusalem
			Paul imprisoned in Caesarea
			Paul travels to Rome
			Martyred in Rome

Footprints of Grace

Let us learn from the lessons on the road to Damascus, about the role of these distinctly different personalities in this event.

1. **God**

    a. **Jesus Initiated the Encounter**—I was initially thinking about who actually started this *Road to Damascus* event. Was it because Saul was persecuting the early Christians that the Lord Jesus appeared, stopping the oppression, and said, *"Saul, Saul, why are you persecuting Me?"* Or did Jesus choose Saul from all the students of the Torah because God saw his zealous fervour to fight and defend Yahweh, and that he was both a Roman citizen and a Jew, fully educated in these two bodies of knowledge? I believe the Lord planned the life of Saul, as Psalm 139 proclaims. I also believe that Jesus' first statement to Saul was to get his immediate attention, as persecuting Christians was preeminent in his mind.

    b. **Jesus Challenged the Existing Status**—Saul's zeal in defending his faith single-mindedly was an expected part of his organisation. You can have a role in a business or a professional endeavour, but at any time, the Lord can disrupt your life by summoning you out of your current state of affairs to do His will. Sometimes we attribute challenging the status quo only to the younger generation, and believe that occupational changes hardly ever occur in the latter stages of one's life. Why enter a disruptive situation when you are already in the calm waters of your life, such as an established career, a well-established company or business, or in retirement? In the past, the Lord has challenged a person's existing condition multiple times. Age is no issue. Think of Abraham, Moses, David, Joseph and many more.

c. **Jesus Said, "Arise and Go"**—When Saul realised to whom he was talking and the authority Jesus embodied, he asked, *"Lord, what do You want me to do?"*
Jesus immediately said, *"Arise and go …"* Like Saul, Jesus also wants us to *move* forward! Jesus will not leave us hanging after an encounter. He wants us to *Arise and Go* to the next point in our journey with Him. God does not want us to be paralysed in His presence or after a consuming experience of the Holy Spirit. He wants us to be active; actively seeking, actively meditating, actively praying, or actively serving. The first steps of this *active pursuit* could be some tiny steps in a new direction. And in these first few steps, you may need some help, just as Saul's companions assisted him in walking to Damascus to meet Ananias.

d. **Jesus Restored Vision and Gave a New Mission**—When the *scales* came off Saul's eyes, his vision was restored, and he also gained a new vision in life. You will see things either differently or more clearly than before. Opportunities may suddenly open, or things that you now perceive were previously unnoticed or overlooked. The loving Words of our Lord in the Bible should open our eyes. For God's *"Word is a lamp to our feet and a light to our path."* Psalm 119:105

2. **Saul**

    a. **Fully Engaged but Ready**—Saul was at the prime of his career, working wholeheartedly in what he believed was his purpose in life. No matter what time or stage you are at in your career, the Lord can summon you at any time; so keep your hands busy and your heart near to God.
    b. **Reverence and a Worshipful Heart**—When we have an exciting encounter with our Saviour, how should we react to this divine event? <u>*With reverence and worship!*</u>

c. **Hearing His Voice**—Sometimes you wish others could have heard the Lord's instructions to you so they would serve as witnesses to the event. While there will be multitudes of *voices* ringing in your heart or constantly trying to get your attention such as social media, notifications, streaming, games, phone calls, calendars, the list goes on; the voice of our Lord should stand out. Not a vague conclusion to incidents and events, but a clear, audible voice through your spirit. Keep in mind to abide in Him.

d. **Acknowledging Authority**—*"Who are you, LORD?"* Saul realised only a heavenly being could initiate such an event, a person worthy of being addressed as LORD. 'The term indicates polite submission.'[21]

e. **Actively Seeking Instructions**—*"Lord, what do You want me to do?"* Humbled by the incident and realising who had just spoken to him, Saul asked further for instructions. Our attitude should be to discover more of God's plan for us.

f. **Spontaneous Prayer and Fasting**—In Saul's experience of *darkness* and waiting, I believe he used this time to reflect, fast and pray. Treat this period as God's *exclusive* time with you. You must believe God is meeting with you in this situation. Take this opportunity to meditate on His Words with prayer and fasting. At this time, the feeling of helplessness will be part of the process. Helplessness allows you to ponder, receive directed solutions, get help with your situation, and exercise your faith.

g. **The New Covenant**—By faith, Saul received the filling of the Holy Spirit, and Ananias baptised him. Being a Pharisaic Jew, Saul's submission was his act of faith.

h. **Acting on the Change**—Saul completed his transformation process when *"at once he began to preach in the*

---

[21] NIV Grace and Truth Study Bible Copyright © 2021 by Zondervan

synagogues that Jesus is the Son of God." Acts 9:20 Faith is credited when you act on it. Knowing what to do is not enough. You need to do what the Lord has instructed you to do. He was still the *same* Saul in many ways, determined, persistent, dedicated, action-driven and goal-oriented, but he had an altered calling. Saul pursued the call. Look at the verb Love. Love is an action word. You have heard it; you know what love is and can even talk about it. But you haven't loved if you do not show or act on love. You may have examined *faith* inside out, studied all the men and women in the Bible who demonstrated *faith* in the finest detail, but unless you dip your feet into the river on the instruction of our Saviour, you haven't exercised faith. Faith is frightening indeed, but the reward of the experience is mind-blowing.

3. **Ananias**

   a. **The Challenging Instructions**—You can imagine Ananias hesitating when Jesus instructed him about Saul. With Saul's reputation as a persecutor of the followers of Jesus, Ananias feared for his life. But the Lord assured Ananias that He had given Saul a new life and direction.
   b. **The Action of Faith**—By faith, Ananias went to see Saul, introduced himself and confirmed the event which had happened to him. Ananias did what Jesus had instructed him to do for Saul.
   c. **The Brotherly Greeting**—Ananias said, *"Brother Saul..."* From an enemy of the believers, Ananias confirmed and acknowledged to Saul that he was now one of them – a follower of Jesus of Nazareth. Isn't this a comforting situation for Saul? An assurance you are not alone and you are forgiven for your past actions. This was more than another chance, but a new life!

4. **The Men who Journeyed with Saul**

    a. **Incidental Witnesses**—No further historical documents were written about these men who travelled with Saul to Damascus. However, the Scriptures mention they witnessed what happened to Saul. They heard the voice and saw the light, but did not see anyone. They served as eyewitnesses to what had happened to Saul on the Road to Damascus. I pray you will not just be *incidental witnesses* to an exceptional event, but you will be the focal point of God's message.

    b. **Led Him by the Hand**—Not only did these men who accompanied Saul witness the incident, but when Saul was told to *"Arise and go..."* they helped Saul reach his destination because he could not see. Having experienced the event, these men knew the voice heralded a special mission for Saul, different from the initial purpose of their journey. You may not be the main focus of God's calling, but when you witness your friend's or companion's calling, or when the Holy Spirit prompts you, are you willing to assist or encourage your brother or sister on their journey? Are you willing to support their calling?

Summary: The Final Thoughts on Paul's Career Change Experience

The Apostle Paul's divine encounter was both dramatic and intense. If it were to happen to any of us today, it would definitely be logged as a mental health issue. One needs a direct and clear intervention from God to shift from a successful and promising career or business. This is what Paul experienced on his way to Damascus.

Dr Peter Tan Chi, the Senior Pastor of CCF (Christ Commission Fellowship, Philippines), has a life story which is a testimony of God's hand in the lives of His children. Here is an account by Albert Jimenez on John 15 Rocks' blog:

As a young man with ambition, God used an incident to change the heart of Peter Tan Chi. Laying helpless in the hospital bed, he asked God to give him another chance in life. In return, he would serve Him. However, the most trying time was still to come for Peter.

The Tan Chi family was one of the rising tycoons in the Philippines in the 1970s until cronyism infected the nation. During the Marcos era, many big companies were forced to be sellouts or be part of the Marcos kleptocracy in the name of expropriation.

The family was neither and they were forced to give up their lucrative business.

The Tan Chi family owned a polyester and chemical plant and the Old Riverside Textile Mills. It was the largest mill in the Philippines. An alleged crony sequestered it during Martial Law, and Peter was fired from the company where he was the vice president.

"I could have become bitter, but I remembered Romans 8:28: 'God causes everything to work together for good to those who love Him.' And I knew I had to make a choice, to be bitter and angry or to trust God. I decided to trust God," he said.

New doors opened, and Peter went into housing development in the 1980s. After martial law, the person who confiscated his father's company was dying. A mutual friend asked Peter to see him.

He was reluctant, but God gave Peter the heart to forgive and even share the Gospel with the man who had stolen their livelihood.

In 1982, Peter started a home Bible study in Brookside Subdivision, Cainta. Only three couples attended the first meeting. They invited others, and soon, the growing 'small group' had to move into the garage to accommodate more people.

Two years later, this became a core group of 40 professional business people who established Christ's Commission Foundation.

In August 1984, they had their first Sunday worship service at the Asian Institute of Management (AIM). The CCF church was born, and Peter became the Senior Pastor.[22]

When the Lord is going to call us, and we are in a comfortable and progressing career or business, a life-defining moment might be necessary to convince us to change our direction. And no matter how subtle or dramatic your change event may be, always trust in the heart of your Master. His loving and faithful hand will guide you through, no matter how hard or hurtful it may be.

Here is a song I would like to share entitled Trust His Heart by Babbie Mason, inspired by the words of Charles Haddon Spurgeon in his sermon, *A Happy Christian:*

> *The worldling blesses God while He gives him plenty,*
> *but the Christian blesses Him when He smites him:*
> *he believes Him to be too wise to err*
> *and too good to be unkind;*
> *he trusts Him where he cannot trace Him,*
> *looks up to Him in the darkest hour,*
> *and believes that all is well.*

Section Questions

1. How would you evaluate your present career or business status?
    a. Very promising
    b. At the peak
    c. Retiring
    d. Coasting
    e. Lost

---

[22]https://www.john15.rocks/testimony-of-peter-tan-chi-pastor-who-leads-by-example/

2. Has the Holy Spirit been prompting you in the area of your career or business recently? Is your current situation being challenged?

3. What miracle can you attribute to your present career situation?

4. Who are the people around you supporting you on your journey?

Additional Resources to the Character

1. John MacArthur has a sermon on Paul's conversion in this <u>video</u> and this <u>transcript</u> entitled *The Astounding Conversion of Paul - Acts 9:1-9*.

2. *Trust His Heart* by Babbie Mason:
https://youtu.be/vQUw53AXlZ0?si=E5WxzmXrx6wqbFxy

3. *The Story of Eric Liddell* – Biography
https://youtu.be/iAA8-13zQCg

4. *The Prayer of Jabez* – Bruce Wilkinson, Multnomah Publishers

5. *The Prayer of Jabez* (Audio) –
https://youtu.be/fEf7pj9i1Aw

6. *It is well with my Soul*, Horatio G. Spafford (1828-1888) -
https://www.umcdiscipleship.org/resources/history-of-hymns-it-is-well-with-my-soul

*But Ruth replied,
'Don't urge me to leave you
or to turn back from you.
Where you go, I will go,
and where you stay, I will stay.
Your people will be my people
and your God my God.
Where you die, I will die,
and there I will be buried.
May the Lord deal with me,
be it ever so severely,
if even death separates you and me.'*

Ruth 1:16-17 (NIVUK)

ITINERARY OF AN IMMIGRANT

A Story of a Migrant

Ruth Chapters 1-4

THE ONLY FEMALE CHARACTER in this series is Ruth. I wanted to understand how our Heavenly Father operated in women's lives in the Scriptures. Our Lord deals with both men and women equally, but looking at the perspective of a female biblical character should be an eye-opener.

Likewise, the approach will be different. We won't look at this case in a narrative structure as presented in the book attributed to her. The Lord led me to look at the life of Ruth and see how events revealed themselves from her perspective.

A Moabite Woman

Ruth lived in a country called Moab, which lay east of the Jordan River. The Moabites were distantly related to the Israelites, being descendants of Abraham's nephew, Lot.

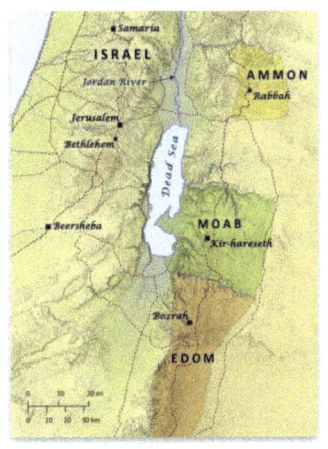

Map Left: Nations Across the Jordan River, Copyright © 2020 by David P. Barrett.

Other than that, no further details are mentioned about Ruth within or without the Scriptures, about her parents, brothers or sisters, her occupation or education. There is no background information on her before her marriage to Mahlon, one of the sons of Elimelech. In fact, the backbone of the book of Ruth is the story of the journey of

Elimelech's family. But she was fortunate being one of only two women whose name was used as the title of a book in the Bible, together with Esther, and as a Gentile woman for that.

I recommend a video produced by Eyewitness Bible Series on The Book of Ruth.[23] It presents an exciting monologue by Ruth. Also, Charles Swindoll has a three-part series[24] on the book of Ruth that can provide a good background on the book and the character.

So, Ruth was an ordinary Moabite woman, living a typical Moabite life in the country of Moab. However, this modest Gentile became the great-grandmother of King David, who was in the line of descendancy to Jesus Christ. What a transformation for a non-Jewish woman. Later, we will see how events transpired that led to her contribution in accomplishing God's overarching plan to save mankind from sin.

Crossroad Encounter

To help understand what caused the changes in Ruth's life, allow me to illustrate in a straight line what could have been the path of Ruth's uninterrupted life in Moab:

Ruth's Life Story

She could have lived her whole life as an average ordinary Moabite woman, marrying a Moabite man, begetting Moabite children, becoming a lovely Moabite grandmother and passing on Moabite traditions and culture to the next generation. Sounds typical, right?

But her straight Moabite life story was altered. She met and got married to a Jewish immigrant named Mahlon. Mahlon's parents were Elimelech and Naomi. His brother's name was Chilion, and he likewise married a Moabite named Orpah. Mahlon's family left Bethlehem in Judah, because of a famine in the land and decided to

---

[23] Kings & Prophets 05 The Book of Ruth: https://youtu.be/KO-GaUVu144
[24] Ruth by Ps Charles Swindoll: https://insight.org/resources/bible/the-historical-books/ruth

move to Moab for a better life. They travelled 80-95 kilometres, approximately a 7-10 days' journey.

Dr David Jeremiah's message on *Ruth Overcoming Bad Decisions*[25] opined that Mahlon's family *could* have made a wrong decision to leave their homeland by *not* seeking the guidance of the Lord before departing. But time and time again, Adonai has proven that no man can obstruct His plan. It is also widely believed that the marriages of both sons were pre-arranged. Most likely, this was agreed upon before Elimelech died, for both of his sons married after their father's death. This is the point at which the two life-story pathways of Ruth and Naomi cross, which disrupted Ruth's life storyline:

However, Ruth's marriage didn't last long. After ten years, both the brothers died for unspecified reasons, making widows of the two Moabite women. Bible commentaries point out that the names of the two Ephrathite brothers illustrate their physical frailty: Mahlon for *sickly* and Chilion for *failing or pining* (Ruth 1:2). This left Ruth's mother-in-law, Naomi, as the only remaining migrant from Bethlehem.

With no other relations in this foreign land, aside from her Moabite daughters-in-law, Naomi made three significant decisions:

1. Go back to the land of Judah,
2. Tell her daughters-in-law to stay in Moab and remarry,
3. Change her name to Mara, which means *bitter*.

According to cultural tradition, Ruth and Orpah were already part of this Jewish family, but Naomi saw that these young ladies would have no pleasant future if they came with her to Judah. She even gave her blessing for them to return to their mother's house, praying

---

[25] Ruth Overcoming Bad Decisions: https://youtu.be/x3WdbTiT1WU

that the Lord would deal kindly with them, as she now believed that the Lord's hand had turned against her.

With this family's tragedies and circumstances, Orpah unreservedly returned to her people and her *gods*. She kissed her mother-in-law goodbye and went back to her own people, but Ruth insisted on staying with Naomi and heading for Bethlehem. Two Moabite ladies in the same sad circumstances, independently made two very different decisions. Both women's lives had changed when they married these immigrants, and yet their dissimilar choices made a further change, as one disappeared into obscurity in Moabite society, while the other was etched into the history of mankind's redemption. Here is Ruth's endearing declaration to Naomi:

> *"Please don't tell me to leave you*
> *and return home!*
> *I will go where you go, I will live where you live;*
> *Your people will be my people,*
> *your God will be my God.*
> *I will die where you die and be buried beside you.*
> *May the Lord punish me if we are ever separated, even*
> *by death!"*

(Contemporary English Version)

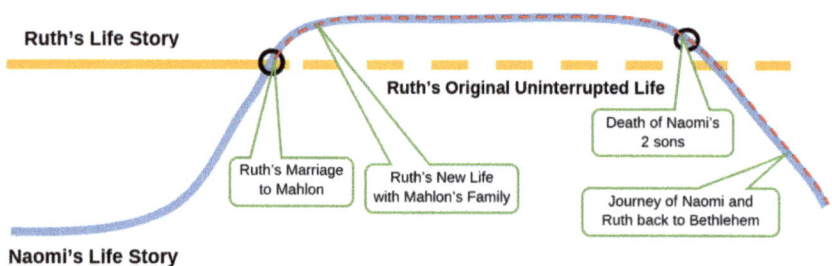

Ruth's marriage into this Jewish family changed which God she worshipped, her values, her people, her loyalty, her priorities, her livelihood, and her perspective; and it changed her.

The Movement

If by any means you are or were an immigrant at any stage, this could be your story.

As I came to this part of my character study, I realised that this had become personal. Most of the messages, reflections, and commentary I encountered on the Book of Ruth were about how romantic the story was; how God beautifully led two individuals from distant origins and different cultures to meet together through God-ordained circumstances, fall in love and, through customary and legal hoops, end up happily ever after.

However, the Holy Spirit showed me another perspective on this story of romance, and that is the plight of an immigrant. Whether to a new city, a new state, or a new country, moving is a significant change in anyone's life. We might be unable to tackle all the different factors and reasons why people migrate, but in this chapter, we will look at what the book of Ruth has revealed about the motive of this movement and how we, as beloved children of our Lord, should respond to these changes. This is the reason I personally relate to Ruth and her story as a migrant.

When Naomi arrived back in Bethlehem, people somewhat doubtfully noticed her. After more than a decade away from her hometown, she was trying to reconnect with her community. This type of movement is called *Return Migration*. I have met several migrants returning to their home country or hometown for various reasons, such as the death of a relative or loved one, or an unsuccessful business venture, or the failure to meet the strict requirements of the host country. Naomi had no husband or son or any other reason to stay in Moab. Likewise, she had heard that the economic downturn in Judah had ended and that growth and expansion were thriving there because the Lord had blessed them again. But Naomi still clung to her sad situation on coming back from Moab, by telling people that her new name was Mara.

Harvesting Growth

It was the beginning of the barley harvest season. Ruth and her mother-in-law came at the right time to migrate back to Bethlehem.

Immigration advisers tell potential migrants that the best time to move is during a region's growth cycle. An economic upturn offers more opportunities and better pay to seekers from within and without the country. And in this modern day, economics is the primary factor for global human movements.

Ruth asked for Naomi's permission before going out to seek *opportunities*. Naomi gave her blessing. Ruth took the opportunity laid out in the Mosaic law in Leviticus 19:9-10 to glean over the heads of barley grain, as she would have been familiar with the Law of Moses after marrying into a Jewish family. The Lord was gracious and had instructed landowners to leave some of the harvest for the needy to gather for themselves. This showed how the Almighty God was full of love and caring for disadvantaged community members (Leviticus 23:22). The blessing helped Ruth and Naomi to settle back in Judah by providing good barley to eat and live off.

Likewise, this barley harvest season also gave Ruth the chance to be noticed by the landowner, Boaz.

When you need to work and gain experience, this also provides an occasion to show what you can do and who you are. Résumés will introduce you to a company's human resources team and hopefully onto the shortlist for the hiring manager to consider. New migrants need to make a double effort to prove themselves worthy. Through God's providence, He had Boaz observe this new migrant in his field. Ruth's positive reputation spread across the workplace, causing Boaz to find favour in her.

An Overview of the Book of Ruth

Ruth	Scenario
Chapter 1	Elimelech and Naomi with their two sons Mahlon and Chilion left Bethlehem, Judah
	Famine is the reason they moved to Moab
	Elimelech died and both sons got married
	Trigger: Ruth Got married to Mahlon.
	After 10 years both of Naomi's sons died
	Naomi asked her daughters-in-law to stay in Moab while she went back to Bethlehem. Only Orpah agreed to stay
	Trigger: Ruth decided to go with Naomi
	Ruth migrated to Bethlehem with Naomi
	Naomi named herself Mara which means 'bitter'.
Chapter 2	**Trigger: Migrated to Bethlehem**
	Ruth worked gleaning heads of the grains in the field owned by Boaz
	Boaz met Ruth and allowed her to glean in his field
	Naomi realised that Boaz was a relative of her husband
Chapter 3 & 4	Naomi advised Ruth about the Jewish culture
	Boaz assured Ruth's redemption
	Judicial proceedings for the redemption of Naomi's land and Ruth
	Boaz is the kinsman redeemer
	Trigger: Boaz took Ruth as his wife.

My Migrant Journey

In 2005, an opportunity came to my family and me to apply for a Work to Residence (WTR) visa in New Zealand. I took thoughtful time in prayer asking for God's leading and a revelation of His will. Migrating would mean leaving my comfort zone, my family and friends, my neighbourhood, and the things I grew up with. I shared this idea with my wife and asked her to pray too. We filed our application with New Zealand Immigration with the help of a registered Christian immigration advisor.

My wife and I continued to pray that His will might be done for my family, and to either open or close the migration door for us. While waiting for a response from Immigration NZ, I completed and gathered all the technical certifications I would need to apply for work once our application was approved. As I was constantly spending time in prayer, God distinctly impressed on me the words He said to Abram,

> *Get out of your country,*
> *From your family*
> *And from your father's house,*
> *To a land that I will show you.* Genesis 12:1

That promise strengthened my spirit, and I looked forward to His journey for us. Similarly, on both sides, our parents said they would give us their blessing if our application was successful.

After a year of waiting, Immigration NZ gave us the signal to start the process, including the paperwork they needed, medical tests and language proficiency. When the Lord opened the door, I began to look for work. One of the chief obstacles in looking for a job in another country is that they require work experience in the host country. They take paper credentials with a grain of salt, so even getting an entry-level job would help for future job opportunities. Just like Ruth, you need to start small, but your experience or reputation will help you get recognised further down the road in your career.

Aside from getting a job, another essential part of the migration journey is a place to stay. I came ahead of my family to Auckland, New Zealand, as we had decided on that action plan, so that while I was looking for a job, expenses would be minimal. I have gone through all the experiences of a new migrant. First, I rented a room, and then purchased my first second-hand car (imagine driving a right-hand-drive manual car after only knowing a left-hand-drive vehicle).

When I landed my first job, I looked for a house to rent for the three of us (my wife, our son and myself, our first child at this stage). I found a two-bedroom granny flat before my wife and son joined me in New Zealand. We got our residency within six months in NZ's Work-to-Residence (WTR) category.

The Kinsman Redeemer

The Mosaic Law on the Kinsman Redeemer was the primary reason for the change in Ruth's life. Scholars believe Boaz was a contemporary of Elimelech, possibly his brother. This was one of the restorative provisions in the law, which Naomi highlighted when she found out where Ruth was gleaning. This was the event Naomi hoped would save them from their disadvantaged circumstances.

Boaz didn't just show favour towards Ruth but was pleased with her. He then told his men to let her glean more barley purposely in his field to show his approval. Recognising Boaz's gesture towards Ruth and her family, Naomi instructed Ruth to approach this matter in a culturally appropriate way to reciprocate such a generous act and fulfil the Law of Moses. When Ruth did what her mother-in-law instructed, Boaz appreciated her action.

Before he assumed his duty as the Kinsman Redeemer, as stated in Leviticus 25:25-28, he knew what the law said: someone was ahead of him in this right, and he had to abide by what the Law stated despite his fascination with Ruth. While the Mosaic Law led the way for this romantic story to progress, it was stipulated in this same Law how to deal with the obstacle so this relationship could be consummated. Boaz must follow the Law and allow the nearest relative of Elimelech to have first option to redeem the property.

Boaz was anxious that, after years of being single, and after someone had finally caught his attention and heart, there was a great possibility he might lose her if the first kinsman-redeemer accepted. When the case of Elimelech was presented to this relative, he agreed to be the kinsman-redeemer.

I can imagine how the heart of Boaz would have sunk when he heard the response. He then laid out the full disclosure that the redemption package also included the widow of Mahlon, Ruth. The close relative stepped back from this privilege to protect his own family's portfolio. He relinquished his rights to being the kinsman redeemer. I am sure Boaz's face glowed with excitement as he received Ruth into his arms legally, also becoming the kinsman-redeemer to all the properties of Elimelech. He fulfilled the Law of Moses to the letter with ten elders as witnesses to this transaction, and personally fulfilled his heart's desire—a relationship made and blessed by God.

The last phase in Ruth's life fell into place as she was to become the great-grandmother of King David, and in a direct line to Jesus, our Lord. The line between Boaz and Ruth intersects because of the Law of the Kinsman Redeemer.

Change Components

As children of the living God, we should be mindful of the events and circumstances around us, as our Lord chooses their seasons and allows them to cross our path. Let us continually and consciously talk to our Father about how these events in our lives contribute to His divine plan for us, as they did in Ruth's life:

1. **Economics**—What actions has the economic environment elicited you to take?
2. **Espousal**—Now that you are joined together in one flesh with your wife or husband, what changes and compromises do you need to make in this relationship?
3. **Eternal Rest**—How has the passing of a loved one affected your future?
4. **Emigration**—What changes must you make or have you made to adapt to a new country?
5. **Endemic Protocols**—How do you act around the governing laws of the land you live in?

Final Thoughts

The Book of Ruth shows us how an inconspicuous gentile woman from Moab named Ruth was taken into marriage by a migrating Jewish family. This event in her life has her name recorded in history as one of the descendants in the line of David and the Messiah. She learned their culture and teachings and embraced Adonai as her own Lord. This changed the course of her destiny and played a vital role in Israel's most prominent king and the birth of our Saviour.

The final diagram shows how the path of each one's life intersects with the others, and that every event point initiated a change incident that altered their lives forever. Without Naomi's migration to Moab, Ruth wouldn't have been brought back to Bethlehem to be redeemed by a prominent law-abiding gentleman named Boaz. Seeing the entire picture of God's plan makes the adventure look dramatic and tremendous, but going through each phase of the journey in detail involves faith as they encounter the struggles and obstacles of their circumstances.

In the end, it was Ruth's faith in the God of Naomi:

> *Please don't tell me to leave you and return home!*
> *I will go where you go, I will live where you live;*
> *your people will be my people, your God will be my God.*
> *I will die where you die and be buried beside you.*
> *May the Lord punish me if we are ever separated, even by death!*

Discussion Questions

1. Do you relate to Ruth as a child of God and being a 'migrant' (either a big move or a small move) to a new place? How would you narrate your "migration" story in the perspective of God's plan for your life?
2. What were your answers to the questions raised in the Change Component section of this chapter?

3. Moving to a new place changes us, for good or otherwise. What are the good and not-so-good changes in your migrant life?
4. Has the Lord asked you to leave your comfort zone to a new area, personally or professionally?

Additional Resource to the Character

1. Listen to Chuck Swindoll's 3-part series on the Book of Ruth: https://insight.org/resources/bible/the-historical-books/ruth

2. Eyewitness Bible Series on The Book of Ruth: https://youtu.be/KO-GaUVu144?si=feDg5d1yHnszSZEF

3. https://www.gotquestions.org/kinsman-redeemer.html

4. David Jeremiah – Ruth: Overcoming Bad Decisions - https://youtu.be/GxN4ErnZqpo

5. John MacArthur – Kinsman Redeemer https://www.gty.org/library/sermons-library/80-238/the-kinsman-redeemer

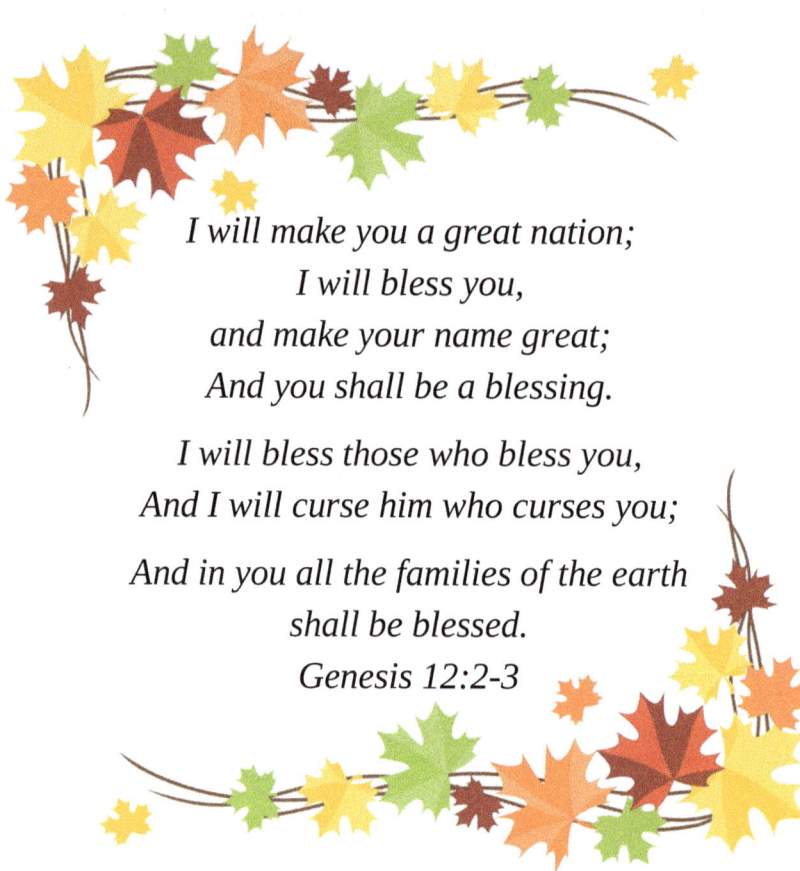

I will make you a great nation;
I will bless you,
and make your name great;
And you shall be a blessing.

I will bless those who bless you,
And I will curse him who curses you;

And in you all the families of the earth
shall be blessed.
Genesis 12:2-3

Driven by a Promise

A Covenant of Change

Y OUR MOTIVATION AND ENTHUSIASM in doing your job, pursuing a career, or running your business are being spurred by hope for a better future, career, and life for you and your family. For Abraham, this was a promise. A promise that took decades to be carried out, and is still being realised today; it was the driving force behind the changes in his life. This agreement overarched his whole life. And this promise, this hope, is more widely known today as the Abrahamic Covenant.

Opening

"And he believed in the Lord, and He (Adonai) accounted it to him for righteousness." (Genesis 15:6)

The Book of Hebrews gives Abraham prominence in its hall of faith – a list in chapter 11. He is also regarded as the '**Father of Faith**' in three major religious groups, namely, Judaism, Christianity, and Islam, which all consider him to have played a pivotal role in the foundation of their faith.

Abraham has most of his life recorded in the Bible, which spans 175 years, and 14 chapters in the book of Genesis (chapters 11-25) which narrates his story. His life was full of ups and downs, loop after loop, twists and turns, sudden stops, and full accelerations. Sounds like a roller-coaster ride! Yes, indeed, his life of faith was like a roller coaster.

And it started with a covenant.

A Binding Contract

The beloved children of the living God are in this relationship because we have a covenant, a contract with our Lord Himself. That is why we have the Old and New Testaments. Testament is another word for covenant. Now we, though Gentiles, are saved, adopted, and redeemed through the blood of Jesus our Saviour, and are bound by this covenant, the Covenant of Grace. *"... that whoever believes in Him should not perish but have everlasting life."* (John 3:16)

In our daily life and ministry, we walk by faith in this world, each with our covenant of faith with our Lord.

Here is the arrangement and the trust between Abraham and God, which is called the Abrahamic Covenant:

Genesis 12:1-3

"Get out of your country,
From your family
And from your father's house,
To a land that I will show you.

I will make you a great nation;
I will bless you
And make your name great;
And you shall be a blessing.

I will bless those who bless you,
And I will curse him who curses you;
And in you all the families of the earth
shall be blessed."

This covenant was initiated to a pagan (Abram worshipped polytheistically), by Almighty God Himself. "Even so God appeared specifically to Abram and gave him (these) personalised instructions."[26] God approached Abram to illustrate pure grace from the Lord.

---

[26] Charles Swindoll, *Abraham: One Nomad's Amazing Journey of Faith* Copyright © 2012, 2014, 2017

What is it all about?

Biblical scholars summarised the covenant into three elements based on the covenantal interactions between God and Abram.

1. Abraham would be given land.
2. Abraham would become a great nation.
3. Abraham and his descendants would be the channel through which the blessings of God would flow to the whole world.

These three elements were recorded in the following passages:

1. Genesis 12:1-3
2. Genesis 15:1-21
3. Genesis 17:1-27

Transformation Points

Here are the highlights of Abraham's life covered in chapters 12-25 of Genesis. We will refer to cross-reference scriptural testimonies to confirm some of these events in his life.

Let us set the scene to introduce Abraham. Abraham's father, Terah, was in the line of Seth, one of the sons of Noah. The name given to him was Abram, *exalted father*. Abram's story starts in the last portion of chapter 11 of Genesis, where it is mentioned that he was married to Sarai. Scripture also said Sarai was barren and as yet, had no child. Abram had a nephew named Lot, the son of his brother, Haran, who had passed away early. So, Terah took on the responsibility of looking after Lot. [Spoiler Alert!] Lot, the nephew, will be a crucial catalyst in several of Abram's change scenarios.

An Overview of the life of Abraham

Age	Phase	Passage	Situation	Change Trigger	Role
0-75	Life with Terah	Genesis 11:27-32	Abram, son of Terah, lived in Ur, Mesapotamia. Married to Sarai and the son of Terah		Son, husband
			Abram's brother Haran died, therefore Terah assumes guardianship of his son Lot		
			Change: From Ur they moved to Haran	Terah decides to	Nomad
			Change: Abram assumes estate and responsibilities	Terah's Death	Patriach
Milestone: The Covenant Conversation. By grace God appeared to Abram and gave him the Abrahamic covenant - Genesis 12:1-3					
75-85 Approx	Nomadic Life	Genesis 12-14	Change: God told Abram to go to Canaan	God	Nomad
			Abram built an altar between Bethel and Ai		Priest
			Famine in Canaan		
			Change: Abram moved to Egypt	Famine	Businessman
			Abram was treated well and prospered		
			Change: God plagued Egypt because Phaoaoh took Sarai. Egyptians found out that Abram deceived them and later sent Abram and his party away	Abram's Deception, Egyptians	Nomad
			Abram moved back to Canaan		
			Change: Abram divided his property and parted ways with Lot	Resource	Estate Manager
			The Lord gave Abram Canaan and he built an altar at Hebron		Priest
			Lot was captured in the war between 9 kingdoms		
			Change: Abram activated his army and rescued Lot	Lot's kidnapping	General
			Melchizedek blessed Abram		
Milestone: The Covenant Conversation. God reaffirms His covenant to Abram as a great nation and signs the covenant - Genesis 15					
86-98 Approx	Birth of a Nation	Genesis 16	Birth of Ishmael	Ishmael	Father
Milestone: The Covenant Conversation. God reaffirms His covenant to Abram as Abram seals it with circumcision and name change to Abraham and Sarah - Genesis 17					
99-175	Living in the covenant and fulfilment of the promise	Genesis 18-25	The Lord promised a son to Abraham and Sarah		
			Abraham negotiated on behalf of Sodom where Lot lived	Lot's life in danger	Negotiator
			Angel rescued Lot and his family and then destroyed Sodom		
			Change: Abraham and his household moved to Gerar	Unconfirmed reasons	Nomad
			Birth of Isaac and Hagar and Ishmael were sent away	Realisation of the promise	Father
			Abraham made a covenant with Abimelech	Security and resources	Promise Keeper
			Abraham passed the test of faith as God commanded him to sacrifice Isaac	God	Father of Faith
			Death of Sarah		Husband
			Abraham found a bride for Isaac		Father
			Abraham remarried		
			Death of Abraham		

A Faithful Follower

Abram's first career change came when Terah migrated up to Haran from Ur of the Chaldeans, now known as Tell el-Muqayyar, travelling approximately 1,127 km (700 miles) alongside the Euphrates River. Ur, a well-established civilisation at that time, became home for a well-settled Abram and the household of Terah. He and his wife, Sarai, and his nephew, Lot, uprooted their lives in Ur and lived as nomads following his father's plan to go to Canaan. But their caravan of possessions and ménage ended up settling at Haran instead. Genesis 11:31-32

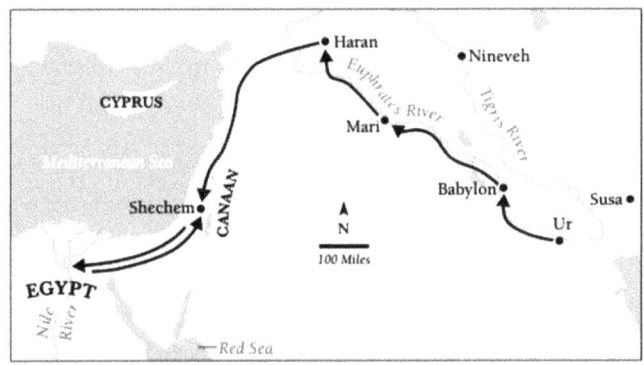

Copyright © 2012, 2014, 2017 ABRAHAM: ONE NOMAD'S AMAZING JOURNEY OF FAITH A Patriarch in Panorama Charles R. Swindoll.

Like Abram, circumstances can affect a parent's decision to move to another city or country, or to venture into a new business, or as a head of an organisation, to decide to sell or merge their company. These decisions will have a significant impact on a family or an organisation. Being a good son or daughter, or member of the clan, your cooperation and contribution to the family business are essential to its continuing success and the security of your children's future.

In an organisation, you are expected to be professional in your role for the continuance of the company or business, whatever the decision of the leadership is and wherever it would take the establishment. These changes will definitely affect you and your role or tasks going forward. You may assume a new position or responsibilities in which the new environment may require all organisation members to participate for the business to succeed. As a professional, you may be offered a new position in the amalgamated company or with the new owners. These organisational changes sometimes prompt employees to rethink and re-evaluate their current careers.

Heritage Transition

The next significant change in Abram's role was when Terah died (Genesis 11:32). He now assumed the primary patriarchal position in the clan of Terah. He was directly responsible for the well-being of the entire household and was now the leader of the whole party that migrated out of Ur. He was also accountable for all the assets left behind by his father.

Was there a situation in your professional career where you were suddenly assigned as an OIC (Officer-in-charge – a person in a temporary leading role) because someone had vacated? The reason for the person leaving could be anything from maternity leave, to finding a new challenge somewhere else.

Likewise, you will begin a new role when you start a family. From a life of being single, you are now responsible for the lives of other human beings aside from yourself. Other well-knit families are more structured as the clan looks to their elders to take the lead. Like in Abram's family, the member in succession assumed the guardianship role when the eldest passed away.

Pathway to Divine Agreement

Genesis 12 lays out what we now call the Abrahamic Covenant. However, it is exciting to know how these events occurred chronologically, specifically when Stephen addressed his audience in Acts 7:2-8 on the calling of Abram. *"The God of glory appeared to our father Abraham in Mesopotamia, before he dwelt in Haran..."*. There at Ur, presumably, is where Abram first received his instructions from God to leave Ur. *"Then he came out of the land of the Chaldeans and dwelt in Haran. And from there, when his father was dead, He moved him to this land in which you now dwell (Canaan)."*

Some scholars also suggest that this might be the reason Terah decided to migrate to Canaan (Genesis 11:31) and ended up in Haran. Abram may have shared with his father the instructions the Lord had given him, which might have convinced him to relocate. And there, in Haran, the covenant details were laid out to Abram after Terah's death.

Do you think Abram would have lasted the long journey or even left Ur without the revelation and command of God? Can you create, maintain, and endure a call, a ministry or a venture without the blessings and promises of our Heavenly Father? I keep a notebook handy to write down passages where the Lord has spoken to me so I can go back to them and assure myself of the promises He has given me in my journey. This little habit has inspired me to start designing an app to help my brothers and sisters in Christ keep track of their promises from God. I hope and pray that this project can come to fruition. Do you have a personal 'covenant' or promise from God to keep you going on your journey? Memorise it! Write it down. Have a unique method to document these blessings.

The Land of Blessings

God led Abram and his party to the region of Canaan, and God confirmed that Canaan was the land He had promised. *"To your descendants I will give this land."* Genesis 12:7. Abram pitched his tent and built an altar between Bethel and Ai, then travelled to the Negev in the southern part of the region. "Abram moved toward the Negev to a less desirable area for raising crops but better for his vocation as a herdsman, perhaps engaging also in merchant activity."[27] Now Abram was in the land which God had promised to give to his descendants.

---

[27] NKJV MacArthur Study Bible. Copyright © 1997, 2006, 2019 by Thomas Nelson.

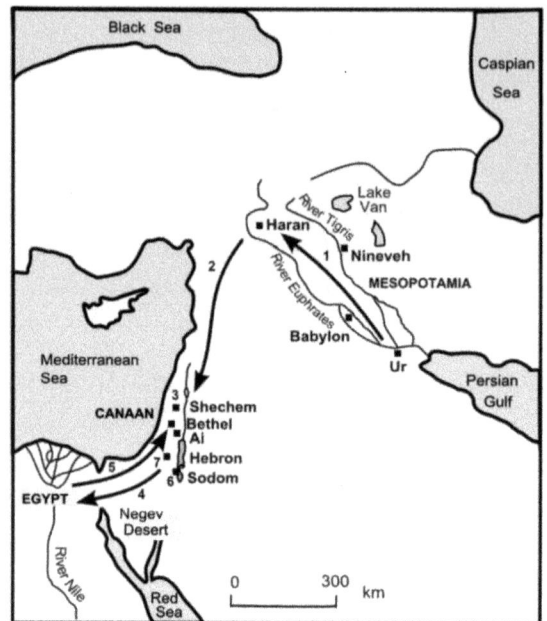

Abram's Journey to Canaan[28]

Stop and take a moment to absorb this. Imagine you are Abram. You have finally settled in a new location after several years of travel from Haran to Canaan. Your personal belongings have now become permanent in your residence's real estate. You have arranged things where you want them to be and now have a place to call HOME. You have moved or migrated from one location to another to finally find an excellent land to grow your livelihood.

You have witnessed the realisation of the first part of the covenant the Lord gave—the promised land—and now you eagerly await the exciting fulfilment of the subsequent item of the agreement, *having your offspring*!

Settled?

Exodus of Hunger

When you are about to wind up for a big batting session by exploiting your vocational asset in a new place after years on the road,

---

[28] https://www.thebiblejourney.org/biblejourney2/23-the-journeys-of-adam-enoch-noah-abraham/abrams-journey-to-canaan/

suddenly, life throws you a giant curve ball. Canaan experienced a natural disaster, a famine.

In today's environment, several factors could contribute to such a catastrophe, when a district encounters this devastation called famine—things like the ecosystem, politics, overpopulation, etc. But back in the time of Abram, most often, nature was the primary cause. As a herdsman, vegetation for his flock was essential, and when the ground could not produce, the absence or lack of water was the culprit. Famine threatens the well-being of the tribe. Therefore, Abram opted to move to neighbouring Egypt.

Whenever the area we live in is going through an economic downturn, moving to a more stable or prosperous location is instinctive. This is true in third-world countries where there may be a sufficient supply of human resources or skills, but opportunities are lacking in their own nation, or more training is required in the host country to obtain a job.

In Egypt, Abram was able to acquire more assets for his household and escape the terror of famine.

The Deceiver's Dilemma

The assets Abram gained in Egypt have a dark story behind their acquisition. The Pharoah of Egypt gifted Abram livestock and servants in return for Sarai. But it exposed Abram's deception towards Pharoah, as he claimed Sarai was his sister and not his wife. Because Sarai had a *"beautiful countenance,"* Abram feared for his life when they entered Egypt. If the authorities knew Abram was this stunning woman's husband, he believed they would kill him to seize her. This trickery was discovered when the entire household of Pharoah was infected with the plague. The Bible said it was a *"great plague,"* so Pharoah commanded his men to send Abram and his entire family out of Egypt.

Another aspect that triggers a change in our career is when others discover things or information we didn't disclose, or a purposeful deception when listing one's credentials, skills, knowledge, or connections. One reason we might do this is that we focus so much on the outcome, such as obtaining the job or position we want, rather than prioritising the character of honesty, reality, or truth about ourselves and being upfront. As for any act of ruse, this cannot be hidden forever. Even the ungodly need honesty in their ranks for their organisation to succeed. Any deceptive action based on company policy, the law of the land, culture, or decorum will eventually have a disastrous effect on one's career.

Stones of Remembrance

After being banished from Egypt by Pharoah, Abram and his party returned to Canaan. Even with the harsh expulsion, he became *"very rich in livestock, in silver, and in gold."* (Genesis 13:2) from his dealings during their stay in Egypt. He returned to where he had built an altar between Bethel and Ai, where he *"called on the name of the Lord."*

To Abram, the altar is a milestone, a reminder of significant interaction with the Lord. A place and a structure that will remind him and his kin and the future generations whom God had promised as his descendants, of how Yahweh kept His promise and blessed him.

Today, as adopted sons and daughters of God, we must establish this practice of building *altars* on our journey with our Lord. We need to record these milestones, to document the conversations and the blessings that our loving Heavenly Father has given us. When we recall these events, we recapture the refreshing anointment of the Holy Spirit. I journal the passages the Spirit gives each day and the personal messages I receive. When the troughs of the journey come, these milestones will arise to help us and strengthen us back on the path of our pilgrimage.

Abram now encountered a situation that big companies and corporations similarly face today when businesses grow too big—large organisations may split up into two or more independent entities. All the economic factors are there that prompt such actions.

1. Overgrowth
2. Scarcity of resources
3. Unhealthy internal competition

Lot, Abram's nephew, also had his flocks, herds and tents. The demand on resources stressed the land. Likewise, the staff working for the two groups were getting under each other's skin, which is not healthy in an organisation, much less in a family.

As an outstanding leader, Abram initiated the solution: *"Please let there be no strife between you and me, and between my herdsmen and your herdsmen; for we are brethren. Is not the whole land before you? Please separate from me. If you take the left, then I will go to the right; or, if you go to the right, then I will go to the left."* Genesis 13:8-9. Lot chose the better of the two (from a human perspective), the plain of Jordan, while Abram dwelt in Canaan, and God blessed him.

Abram built another altar in Hebron.

Has the Lord spoken to you? If His Spirit has spoken to you, write it down and worship the Lord. Add another milestone in your journey.

The General

Lot chose the plain of Jordan because it was *"like the garden of the Lord, like the land of Egypt as you go toward Zoar."* A well-watered land for his domesticated animals. Modern and advanced, the land lured Lot, and he enjoyed the lifestyle that matched his wealth in the vibrant, established cities on the savanna. He willingly moved and established his home closer to Sodom.

In an unfortunate event, the King of Sodom joined the war in what is famously known in the Bible as the War of the Nine Kingdoms in Genesis 14. During this conflict, the conquering armies captured and divested Sodom of all its goods and people, also taking Lot and his household captive.

Abram heard this atrocious news about his nephew from someone who escaped the horrific attack on Sodom. His concern for Lot evoked anger in Abram and he mobilised his 318 armed and trained men to track down the perpetrators. With Abram's strategic acumen, they recaptured all the goods and rescued his beloved nephew, Lot. Loyalty to family was vital to Abram. Scripture may not have explicitly recorded that in Abram's household, he maintained an army. Still, scholars believe that having such an extensive holding of livestock and precious metals required Abram to maintain capable protection to safeguard his estate. Faced with threat and danger, Abram transformed from a settled farmer to a fearsome army general.

Family is also precious and close to our hearts, and we intentionally adapt to prevailing circumstances to help and support them. We would be willing to change to serve, save, protect and provide for our loved ones. Do you see yourself in a situation where you need to change careers or take a job because of your family's needs?

Here's a story, one of hundreds of similar stories of OFW (Overseas Filipino Workers) working around the globe, changing their original careers to support their families back home:

Corazon, or Cora, was an accountant in her home country. She had a good job and stable income but needed more than her current salary. She looked for opportunities abroad. After some research, she found a job as a domestic helper in Hong Kong and applied for it. Even though she had to leave her profession and skills behind and adapt to a new culture, the job offered her a higher salary and the opportunity to provide for her family in the Philippines. She was able to use her organisational skills and attention to detail to excel in her new role as a domestic helper.

Divine Wisdom

Genesis 14:17-24 perfectly transcribes what transpired in Abram's meeting with Melchizedek, the Priest-King of God Most High and King of Salem; and Bera, king of Sodom. Bera hurriedly went out to meet Abram and his troops, hoping to get a favourable early deal with the victor, like buyers going early in the morning to get the best and freshest catch or harvest in the market.

Before any negotiations were entered into, and at Abram's complete discretion, he gave a tithe of the spoils to Melchizedek in the worship of the Lord. In return, the Priest-King blessed Abram:

> *Blessed be Abram of God Most High,*
> *Possessor of heaven and earth;*
> *And blessed be God Most High,*
> *Who has delivered your enemies into your hand.*
> Genesis 14:19-20

But Abram rejected Bera's proposal that he keep all the remaining captured goods for himself while the king of Sodom received back only his own people. Abram did not want the goods in case Bera claimed that he had made Abram rich, rather than God. There was one proviso, though. Because of his unselfish and astute leadership, Abram compassionately considered his troops, who had sacrificed themselves when they undertook this assignment to rescue Lot. He negotiated on their behalf to get their portion of the possessions.

When you are close to the Lord, you will be guided accordingly on managing or distributing the resources He has blessed you with through your business, job, or career.

> *When wisdom enters your heart,*
> *And knowledge is pleasant to your soul,*
> *Discretion will preserve you;*
> *Understanding will keep you,*
> *To deliver you from the way of evil,*
> *From the man who speaks perverse things.*
> Proverbs 2:10-12

Affirmation

God reaffirms His covenant with Abram in a vision. He reminded Abram again of his promise and affixed His 'signature', or solemnised the covenant. The procedure elaborated in Genesis 15 is an ancient way to seal an agreement.

Has the Lord been trying to tell you to take Him at His word which He has revealed personally to you? I challenge you to take that solemn and worshipful time alone to intimately talk to your Saviour and listen to His gentle voice. Write the promises He has presented to you. Take Him at His word and keep them in your heart. In my special notebook, I have diligently written down these precious promises I have received, which the Holy Spirit directed me to as His personal message to me. I encourage you to spend that valuable moment with the Lord.

Personalise this statement from God to you:

Do not be afraid, _____.

I am your shield, your exceedingly great reward.

MY PRAYER FOR YOU:

*Oh Lord, the God of Abraham,
Isaac and Jacob,
Please bless my brother/sister as they come
humbly before you. Bless them with Your presence.
Bless them with the promises in Your Word.
Strengthen their faith to trust You more.
In the name of our beloved Saviour Jesus, Amen.*

Progenitorship

Abram became a father. This stage of one's life is genuinely transformational and challenging. However, this incident was not how the Most High wanted the story to be played out. Abram became the father of his first son, Ishmael, through Sarai's maidservant, Haggai. Sometimes, we misunderstand how God intends to realise His promises to us, and at times, we determine how it should play out, as was the case with Sarai. She believed the Lord would fulfil His promise to Abram for a great nation, and knowing her barrenness, she thought her solution was part of His plan. The Lord corrected Abram earlier when he suggested a legal remedy as to how God would realise His promise (Genesis 15:2-6). The Lord's words were clear and precise. As mortals and sinners, we like to intervene. Through this well-intended intervention, centuries, and generations of animosity between the Jews and the Arabs still prevails today.

Abraham and Sarah

The Lord Yahweh now appeared to Abram for the third time, and this time the meeting and the conversation would significantly impact Abram's legacy. In this interaction, God explicitly revealed the promise He gave to Abram concerning his descendants. The first change was Abram's name. Abram would now be known as Abraham: *Father of a Multitude*. And Sarai would also have a new name, Sarah: *Princess*.

And God said to Abraham: *"As for you, you shall keep My covenant, you and your descendants after you throughout their generations."* Genesis 17:9. Abraham's part of the covenant was to apply the physical circumcision to all male members of his household and to the generations to come, for *"My covenant shall be in your flesh for an everlasting covenant."*

A covenant in the Old Testament is a legally binding obligation between two parties, God and man, and God often initiated these for man's redemption.

Do you have a personal covenant with the Lord? What are the promises, and what are His conditions?

Strategic Persuasion

Another masterful expertise Abraham had was his astute negotiating skills. Abraham's aptitude came into play when he learned from the three supernatural visitors that God would destroy Sodom because of their wicked and violent lifestyle. And guess what? Lot and his household were still living there. As the surviving senior member of the clan, Abraham's affinity for Lot and his inherent sense of responsibility to his nephew kicked in again.

"Would You also destroy the righteous with the wicked?" Abraham asked.

Abraham started the negotiations.

...50 righteous? The Lord agreed not to send down judgement.

...45 righteous? The Lord agreed.

...40 righteous? The Lord agreed.

...30 righteous? The Lord agreed.

...20 righteous? The Lord agreed.

...10 righteous? *"I will not destroy it (Sodom) for the sake of ten."*

The angels only found Lot and his immediate family righteous in the cities of the plain. By faith, Abraham had used his intercessory talents to save Lot from obliteration.

Take an inventory of the skills you have learned throughout your professional or business life. The Lord will use them for His kingdom when the opportunity arises.

Nomadic Lifestyle

Abraham packed up his tents and began his nomadic life again. This time to Gerar, a Philistine city on the border between Canaan and Egypt whose king was Abimelech. Again, Abraham repeated his old trick from Egypt by introducing Sarah as his sister and not his wife. This made Abimelech able to take Sarah into his palace as his own. But God told Abimelech in a dream that *"he is a dead man"* by taking another man's wife.

Subsequently, God said He protected Abimelech from sinning, and told the king to restore Sarah to the prophet Abraham. Yes, a prophet! This is the first time God addressed him as a prophet and identified him as one. A prophet is a spokesman for God, and he speaks in the name and authority of God. Therefore, in all those years that Abraham was interacting with Yahweh and living out God's covenant with him, he was actually in a career, being a prophet.

Back to the entanglement that Abraham created with Abimelech. Abimelech confronted Abraham who gave his excuse, *"Because I thought, surely the fear of God is not in this place; and they will kill me on account of my wife."* Such presumptions could have killed the king! In the king's act of restoration, he gave *"sheep, oxen, and male and female servants…"* to Abraham's estate, and also land to dwell in; and a thousand pieces of silver! In return, Abraham prayed to God, and God healed the king, his wife and all the king's female servants, for their wombs had been closed because of this incident.

The Promise Fulfilled

Abraham became a father again, and this time through the womb of Sarah, the realisation of the covenant God made between them. Though I do not advocate favouritism among siblings, this is how much loved the baby boy was by the 100-year-old patriarch. Fatherhood is likewise a career like the mum's, especially in the early years of the baby's life.

As a father, Abraham was also full of love, joy, hope toward his first son, Ishmael, by Haggai. He bonded well with Ishmael, but felt distressed when Sarah told him to banish the mother and her son. Sarah became uncomfortable with the boy's reaction to her own son. But God instructed Abraham to comply with Sarah's demands. God promised to look after the two boys and make a nation through Ishmael also.

With a heavy heart in the early morning, Abraham, as a loving father, made as many provisions as he could prepare for both Haggai and Ishmael before sending them away.

At the most desperate point of their journey, the Angel of the Lord came to them in the desert and attended to their needs. The Lord was faithful to His promises.

A Promise Keeper

Abraham, Abimelech and Phichol (the commander of Abimelech's army), held a summit together. The king of Gerar instigated this meeting to assure himself that no harm now or in the future would fall upon him and his offspring.

Abraham promised.

Abraham took the opportunity to raise an issue with Abimelech involving a well he had built which had been seized by the king's men. Having no knowledge of this incursion, Abimelech agreed to have the well included in the covenant among equals. Thus, the place was called Beersheba – Well of Oath, or Well of the Seven.

Covenants, treaties, agreements, and contracts are the terms we use today to seal or complete an understanding between two or more parties. When we have concurred with someone in good faith and with due diligence, we must do what was agreed upon and keep our word to the other party.

Working as a contractor for several organisations, I learned to carefully read each contract I signed. This document lists our responsibilities and liabilities, the compensation and the product or services required in the exchange. In this fast-paced society, sometimes these contracts need to be improved. On occasions, old contracts are copied and pasted into new contracts. Some still bear the name of the contractor from which this new contract was copied. From time to time, I discovered the finer details of the job description needed to be returned to the employer for clarification or correction. But when the contract has been signed, we need to keep our word and fulfil our part of the agreement.

The Lord is the Everlasting God who keeps his promises. As Nehemiah prayed:

> *"I pray, Lord God of heaven,*
> *O great and awesome God, You who keep Your*
> *covenant and mercy with those who love You and*
> *observe Your commandments...."*

Faith Under the Knife

God asked Abraham to offer his beloved son, the eagerly awaited embodiment of the covenant given many years prior. However, the book of Genesis does not elaborate on the mental stress Abraham must have been going through in carrying out the instruction of the God he trusted and loved, to slay as a sacrifice his cherished son. This oft-told event in the Scriptures is where Abraham became regarded as the Father of Faith.

Walk through your mind as you read Genesis 22:1-19: *"Take your son, your only son, whom you love..."*

This test that Abraham went through was a specific directive for him and him only. There were four people involved in this process, or five, as I would include Sarah. I believe Abraham would have told her what this journey was about since they would be away for approximately six to eight days, but no one knew, except for Abraham, the details of this mission. This was strictly between God and Abraham and should never be taken as an instruction outside of this scenario. God explicitly forbids child sacrifice. The idea did not even enter His mind (Leviticus 20:2-5, Jeremiah 19:5).

In your jobs, careers, or businesses you are and will be scrutinised as children of the Lord Most High. The world will constantly examine your faith. Like Joseph, your integrity will be tested in the marketplace in times of success, or when holding a significant position in a company. Like Job, his entire household and estate were decimated, but he never gave up his loyalty to the one true God.

You might be given one, two, or five bags of gold; what yield will you give back to the Master? The parable lays out the rewards and penalties of the returns. But our Lord is merciful, gracious, and willing to bless as He challenges the faith of His people with this familiar promise in Malachi 3:10

> "Bring the whole tithe into the storehouse, that there may be food in my house. Test me in this,' says the Lord Almighty, 'and see if I will not throw open the floodgates of heaven and pour out so much blessing that there will not be room enough to store it."
> (NIVUK)

When the Lord provides you with a great job, a satisfying career, or a prosperous and thriving business, in this success, He uses this success to challenge your faith in Him. He will ensure that these blessings from Him will not stand in the way of your relationship with Him. As an omniscient God, He knew beforehand that Abraham's faith would exceed the challenge. This test is *for* Abraham to see, experience, and learn from for the benefit of the succeeding generations.

Pray that we will stand true and find ourselves approved by our King.

Conclusion Regarding Abraham

The following three chapters of Genesis, 23–25, wind up the rollercoaster ride of Abraham's life of faith and his covenant with God. Though the events in the latter years of his life would not be as career-altering as the previous years, they would still be as significant in any of our lives as they were to him. And you can count on Abraham to make his life of faith finale a smash!

Abraham's career of faith continues even in the saddest part of his life, the death of his beloved Sarah. Being together for at least 67 years, going through Abraham's journey of commitment to Yahweh God, and giving birth to the nation of Israel, Sarah, with her beautiful countenance, finally said goodbye to her dearest at 127 years of age. As part of his role, it was his spousal duty to lay her body to rest in a suitable place. Being a foreigner in the land that was promised to him, he didn't own any land. So, he asked Ephron if he could buy his land for a burial site to lay Sarah's body. Likewise, purchasing the land ensured his own eventual resting place, an essential characteristic of a businessman.

Abraham then also fulfilled his patriarchal responsibility by looking for a wife for Isaac. To accomplish this, Isaac's wife should belong to his original clan. Due to his old age, he must execute this duty remotely (remember this was customary in Old Testament times!). He gave a charge to his senior servant to go back to Mesopotamia with gifts to find an appropriate bride for his son. This trusted servant was led miraculously to Rebekah, the granddaughter of Nahor, Abraham's brother (Genesis 11:27).

She was then brought back to Isaac, and the servant narrated the amazing events that fell into order to assure him that she was precisely the one to bring home. *"So, she became his wife, and he loved her; and Isaac was comforted after his mother's death."* Genesis 24:67 NIVUK

Abraham also remarried and took Keturah as his wife, and Abraham had more children with her. As the patriarch, Abraham *"gave all he had to Isaac"*, but as a father, he gave gifts to his sons through Keturah and other concubines.

"Then Abraham breathed his last and died in a good old age" of 175 years. Even Ishmael returned and, together with Isaac, paid their last respects, and laid their father beside Sarah, his wife, to rest inside the burial-site cave.

This was the end of the journey of faith and career of Abraham.

Section Summary

Abraham's life was full of changes—from moving across the region as a nomad to becoming an army commander; from a childless father to a patriarch of two great nations; from a pagan believer to the father of faith. Abraham went through all these changes because they were based on the promise given to him by Almighty God, called the Abrahamic Covenant.

Section Questions

1. What personal promises have you received from God?

2. What milestones have you gone through in your journey with the Lord? Have you recorded these milestones and established a written altar to commemorate that event?

3. Has an economic or social condition made you change or consider changing your career or profession?

Additional Resource to the Character

"Abraham" by Charles R. Swindoll – Ch. 1.
https://youtu.be/5y1hyunmz08
Genesis & Job 08 Abraham – Eyewitness Bible Series
https://youtu.be/LbAWpvkQeRo

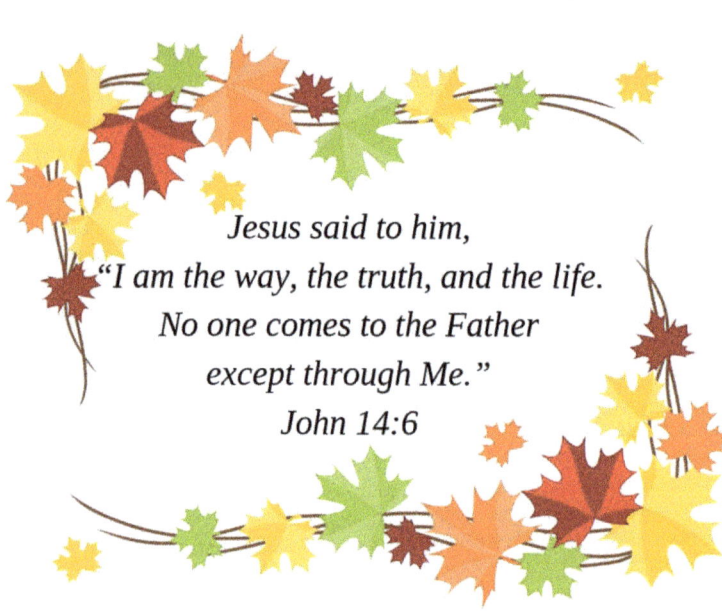

*Jesus said to him,
"I am the way, the truth, and the life.
No one comes to the Father
except through Me."
John 14:6*

Foreknowledge

He Foreknew, Yet...

THE LIFE OF JESUS gives us a unique character to study on how change occurs in one's life, and this is a challenge I want to take with you on this journey. More specifically, His career change, for *He knew beforehand* His rightful identity, where the events in His life would take place, and why He was here in human form.

This chapter looks at the perspective of His humanity as it plays out, as the central theme when exploring these changes. We appreciate that these events occurred in concurrence with His divinity. So why would I include a divine character? Good question! Here in the Bible, we are challenged to:

> *Adopt the same attitude as that of Christ Jesus,*
> *who, existing in the form of God,*
> *did not consider equality with God*
> *as something to be exploited.*
> *Instead, he emptied himself*
> *by assuming the form of a servant,*
> *taking on the likeness of humanity.*
> *And when he had come as a man,*
> *he humbled himself by becoming obedient*
> *to the point of death—*
> *even to death on a cross.*
> Philippians 2:5-8 (CSB)

> *For we do not have a high priest who is unable to*
> *sympathize with our weaknesses, but one who has*
> *been tempted in every way as we are, yet without sin.*
> Hebrews 4:15 (CSB)

Jesus showed us how to face these circumstances at every turn.

So, what does Jesus foreknow about Himself? He knew who His real Father was. He knew what His purpose here on Earth was. He knew what His real business here was. He knew what God's kingdom was. He knew what He could do. He knew who the people were that He would select to follow Him, and who would eventually betray Him. He knew He needed to obey the Law of Moses. He knew that in His public ministry, He would encounter tremendous opposition and would agitate the High Priests. He knew He would be arrested, persecuted, suffer, and be crucified. He knew who He was, the Messiah, the Holy Lamb of God.

The first four books of the New Testament, called the Gospels, document the life and works of this Man called Jesus of Nazareth. They show us that this Jesus was as human as any of us with His frailties, emotions, limitations, and capabilities, but the testament of His works confirm He is divine.

The Chosen series (running in its fourth season as of 2024) helped me visually connect to the events as narrated by the Gospel writers. I highly recommend this as a supplementary resource to reading the four Gospel books (Matthew, Mark, Luke and John). This series shows an *entertaining* rendition of the life of Christ, but the Holy Scriptures still serve as the ultimate authority on the life of our Saviour. (link in Resources at the end of the chapter)

Another highly recommended video series to better appreciate one of the Gospel books, Luke, is made by Eyewitness Bible Series—the story behind the book according to Luke and Theophilus.

The Promise Unveiled

> *"The voice of one crying in the wilderness:*
> *'Prepare the way of the Lord;*
> *Make straight in the desert*
> *A highway for our God...'"* Isaiah 40:3

Here are two questions to start with:

1. When pursuing a dream or a career, what would you do differently if you knew then what you know now about the success of your job?

2. How would you approach a challenge, or how different would your attitude be if you knew you would not fail?

Why do hindrances arise against a favourable outcome for a professional or business goal? But you know these hindrances would vanish if you knew success was certain. Knowing the endgame from the start also entails responsibility, and extreme caution should be observed when one possesses such knowledge. Jesus had this knowledge.

But in His infinite knowledge and power, the Lord *submitted* willingly to the plans of His Father for mankind, regardless of the unimaginable suffering He would undergo, which He anticipated. You can see this in His prayer in the garden of Gethsemane.

> *"And He was withdrawn from them about a stone's throw, and He knelt down and prayed, saying, 'Father, if it is Your will, take this cup away from Me; nevertheless, not My will, but Yours, be done.' Then an angel appeared to Him from heaven, strengthening Him. And being in agony, He prayed more earnestly. Then His sweat became like great drops of blood falling down to the ground."*
> Luke 22:41-44

The Carpenter's Son

> *"And the Child grew and became strong in spirit, filled with wisdom; and the grace of God was upon Him."*
> Luke 2:40

> *"Then he went down to Nazareth with them and was obedient to them. But his mother treasured all these things in her heart. And Jesus grew in wisdom and stature, and in favour with God and man."*
> Luke 2:51-52

At the age of 12, having the foreknowledge of His life and His true self, Jesus *attended* to His Father's business. Mary noticed this uncharacteristic behaviour of Jesus not staying close to the caravan of travelling Jews leaving Jerusalem after the festival of the Passover. As a loving and obedient son, He cut short His lively interaction with the teachers at the temple to be with His earthly parents. Not only did He foreknow, but He knew His standing at that moment, that His revelation to the public had not yet come.

Carpentry could have been Jesus' profession since His adoptive father, Joseph the Nazarene, was a carpenter by trade. However, for His vocation, Jesus knew He had a higher calling. Though we engage in our career, profession or business, as believers of the Living God, we have a higher calling in His Kingdom and should also be doing our *Father's business*. Jesus knew the dichotomy He had to deal with daily here on Earth.

Jesus exhibited patience in the first 30 years of His life. He was waiting for God's perfect timing to reveal Himself as the promised Messiah.

Galilee's Awakening

The book of Luke says, "... *Jesus Himself began His ministry at about thirty years of age...*" Luke 3:23. The God-Man entity of the Holy Triune God approached His cousin, John the baptiser, requesting that he be immersed by him in the Jordan River to fulfil this act of righteousness that John preached. As Jesus was approaching, His cousin proclaimed, *"Look, the Lamb of God, who takes away the sin of the world!"* John 1:29 Give attention to the mindset of Christ when John said to Him, *"I am the one who needs to be baptized by you, so why are you coming to me?"*

Listen to what Jesus said in response, *"It should be done, for we must carry out all that God requires."* So, John agreed to baptise him (Matthew 3:14-15 NLT), which was an excellent example for all followers of Christ; though He is fully God and fully man, this conversation demonstrated His humility and obedience to the Father – *"for we must carry out all that God requires."* Jesus did not shortcut the process or forsake God's commands for His children. Then John saw the *"Spirit descending from heaven like a dove, and He remained upon Him... 'this is He who baptizes with the Holy Spirit.' And I have seen and testified that this is the Son of God."*

Here are the core components that made this milestone happen, which eventually launched the public ministry of Jesus:

1. His character of *humility*
2. His attitude of *obedience* (water baptism)
3. The *anointing* of the Holy Spirit
4. The *testimonies* of others about Him

Jesus started by calling His disciples and teaching them the Kingdom of Heaven.

Miracles Revealed

Jesus and His first disciples attended a wedding feast held in Cana of Galilee. This is the first recorded public miracle by Jesus, and scholars consider it the beginning of His open ministry. The writer of the Book of John used this event to kick off his detailed witness to the eight miracles recorded in his book giving evidence to the Deity of Jesus Christ.

Jesus attended this wedding with His mother, Mary, who is believed to be related to the couple. The disciples also joined this celebration together with their Rabbi. This was a joyful and celebratory event for the clan. *"Such a wedding celebration in Jewish culture could last for a week."* (J. MacArthur). As the servers in the backroom poured the last few drops from the wine vessels into the serving jars, and knowing the end of the feast was yet to be foreseen, they quickly informed the organising committee of this impending disaster, which would cause a humiliating scenario for the newly-weds' families. Mary was believed to be part of this committee, and instinctively approached the *only* person she knew who could help in this impossible situation, Jesus.

> *"Jesus replied to His mother, 'Woman, what does your concern have to do with Me? My hour has not yet come.' His mother said to the servants, 'Whatever He says to you, do it.'"*

Word went out that something extraordinary had happened at that wedding, and the people who tasted the wine confirmed it to be true. Jesus handled the timing of His disclosure, and let the situation mature into change, and was neither rushed nor forced.

Change can happen at any stage in one's life, possibly earlier, or later. Jesus started His ministry at 30, and this is neither a standard nor an aim for anyone else's transformation. His relationship with the Father prompted Him as to when the process should start.

> *"And truly Jesus did many other signs in the presence of His disciples, which are not written in this book; but these are written that you may believe that Jesus is the Christ, the Son of God, and that believing you may have life in His name."*
> John 20:30-31

Jesus is Risen, Indeed!

After Jesus was crucified, buried, and raised to life, He finally assumed His eternal role as the Saviour of the world, Jesus in glorified form. The Rabbi and teacher of the twelve who came to impart the words of the Father to the world, was now transformed to glory!

> *"And now, O Father, glorify Me together with Yourself, with the glory which I had with You before the world was."* John 17:5

> *"For I have given to them the words which You have given Me; and they have received them, and have known surely that I came forth from You; and they have believed that You sent Me."* John 17:8

Here are His eternal roles:

1. **He is Lord:** *"And Jesus came and spoke to them, saying, 'All authority has been given to Me in heaven and on earth.'"* (Matthew 28:18)

2. **He is King of Kings:** *"And He has on His robe and on His thigh a name written:*

   KING OF KINGS AND
   LORD OF LORDS."
   Revelation 19:16

3. **He is our Mediator:** *"For there is one God and one Mediator between God and men, the Man Christ Jesus."* (1 Timothy 2:5)

4. **He is our High Priest:** *"Seeing then that we have a great High Priest who has passed through the heavens, Jesus the Son of God, let us hold fast our confession. For we do not have a High Priest who cannot sympathize with our weaknesses, but was in all points tempted as we are, yet without sin. Let us therefore come boldly to the throne of grace, that we may obtain mercy and find grace to help in time of need."* (Hebrews 4:14-16)

5. **He is our Advocate:** *"My little children, these things I write to you, so that you may not sin. And if anyone sins, we have an Advocate with the Father, Jesus Christ the righteous."* (1 John 2:1)

6. **He is our Saviour:** *"For God so loved the world that He gave His only begotten Son, that whoever believes in Him should not perish but have everlasting life."* (John 3:16)

Here is also a list of remarkable men and women of our Lord Jesus who have given their lives for the Gospel. By faith, they offered their life of service, not experiencing the full benefit of their labour in their lifetime, but the harvest reaped plenty of souls who came to the saving knowledge of Jesus. Missionaries like: Hudson Taylor, Adoniram Judson, Robert Morrison, John Paton, Eric Liddell, Jim Elliott, David Livingstone, Lottie Moon and more. This shows that one's vocational success is not measured in a lifetime. God's plan covers both an eternity and each individual day within His perfect timing. He calls to change, and with faith, we follow.

"He is no fool who gives what he cannot keep, to gain what he cannot lose." Jim Elliot

Christ is RISEN! He is Risen INDEED!

Jesus Knew, Yet...

Jesus knew beforehand all the things that would happen in His life. He knew His capabilities as a God-Man, His responsibilities, and the timing corresponding to these. He also knew the Father's plan for mankind and was at the centre of it all. But with all His power and authority, He knew He had to live out this life in a frail and finite pod of a human body full of emotions and pain.

In human form, Jesus demonstrated patience, humility, obedience and submission to the will of His Heavenly Father, in situations that could easily crush a human body and spirit. He endured these things because of His love for you and me. Jesus knew He was the Lamb of God who would take away the sin of the world. And our God knows you and the reason why He created you.

Jesus' foreknowledge of Himself revealed personal character qualities and transformational skills:

1. **Humility**—Jesus knew He needed to adhere to the limitations and obligations of His humanity as a son, as a Jew, and as the only begotten Son of God. He must live as a human. He was born and grew in stature, knowledge, and strength as any other child.

2. **Obedience**—Jesus knew He must comply with the statutes set out by God for His people and the fulfilment of all righteousness.
3. **Discernment**—Jesus knew the right people who would be His disciples.
4. **Submission**—Jesus knew He would be betrayed, arrested, tortured, and crucified. Despite that, He submitted to God's perfect will.
5. **Loving Relationship**—Jesus knew the Father, and the Father knew Him.
6. **Change Management**—Jesus knew He was the Change catalyst, but He allowed the process to go by God's timing.
7. **Managing Expectations**—Jesus knew the reality of God's Kingdom.
8. **Time Management**—Jesus knew the right time to act.
9. **Problem Management**—Jesus knew His message would face opposition from the people in authority.
10. **People Management**—Jesus knew His power, yet He let things play out for people to exercise their faith, and allowed them to take part in His miracles.

Now, it was not only Jesus who knew who He was, and His purpose and destiny here on Earth. There were others to whom the Lord also revealed His identity early on: Mary knew, Joseph knew, and others received this divine revelation and knew His role in the salvation of mankind.

1. Shepherds who worshipped Him in the feeding trough,
2. The wise men from the East,
3. John the Baptiser,
4. Simeon (Luke 2:25),
5. Anna, the daughter of Penuel (Luke 2:36),
6. Zechariah and Elizabeth, parents of John the Baptiser.

Do you have this intimate relationship with Jesus?

I encourage you to have this amazing relationship with the Saviour, the lover of your soul. Jesus is waiting for you in your prayer closet. Then the Holy Spirit will always be there beside you to guide you every day.

> *"However, when He, the Spirit of truth, has come, He will guide you into all truth; for He will not speak on His own authority, but whatever He hears He will speak; and He will tell you things to come."*
>
> John 16:13

Overview of the Life of Jesus

Age	Period	Passage	Scenario
0-30	Pre-Ministry years	The Gospels	Born in Bethlehem though Mary
			Jesus was dedicated and circumcised in the Temple
			Escaped to Egypt
			Returned to Nazareth after the death of Herod
			Raised by Joseph and Mary
			At 12 years old, Jesus visited the Temple and was left behind and later found conversing with the teachers.
			Approached and met with John the baptiser at the River Jordan
Catalyst: Confirmation and baptism by John the baptiser. His time has come.			
30-33	Ministry years	The Gospels	Temptation in the wilderness
			Meets His first disciples
			First miracle at Cana
			Rest of the disciples chosen
			Sermon on the mount
			Jesus calmed the storm
			Fed the 5000
			Jesus walked on water
			Transfiguration of Jesus
			Lazarus raised
			The Last Supper
			Prayer in the garden
			Jesus was arrested
			Jesus was judged, crucified and buried
Catalyst: Resurrected and ascended to the right hand of God			

Section Questions:

1. What character qualities or attitudes of Christ in His humanity do you need for your transformation process?

2. Has our Heavenly Father called you to, or revealed to you, a new career you need or will transform into?

3. What items are needed outside of yourself, whether material, circumstantial, environmental, or relational, to help progress the change process?

4. Have you come to the saving knowledge of Jesus Christ our Lord? If not, ask Him to forgive your sins, repent and accept Him as your Lord.

Additional Resources

Eyewitness Bible Series. https://eyewitnesbible.org
Here is the Eyewitness account of Luke and Theophilus.
https://youtu.be/nE28gY4jz8A

The Chosen series - https://watch.thechosen.tv/

Keith Green: Oh Lord, You're Beautiful
https://youtu.be/tqEa1Uo9UZc

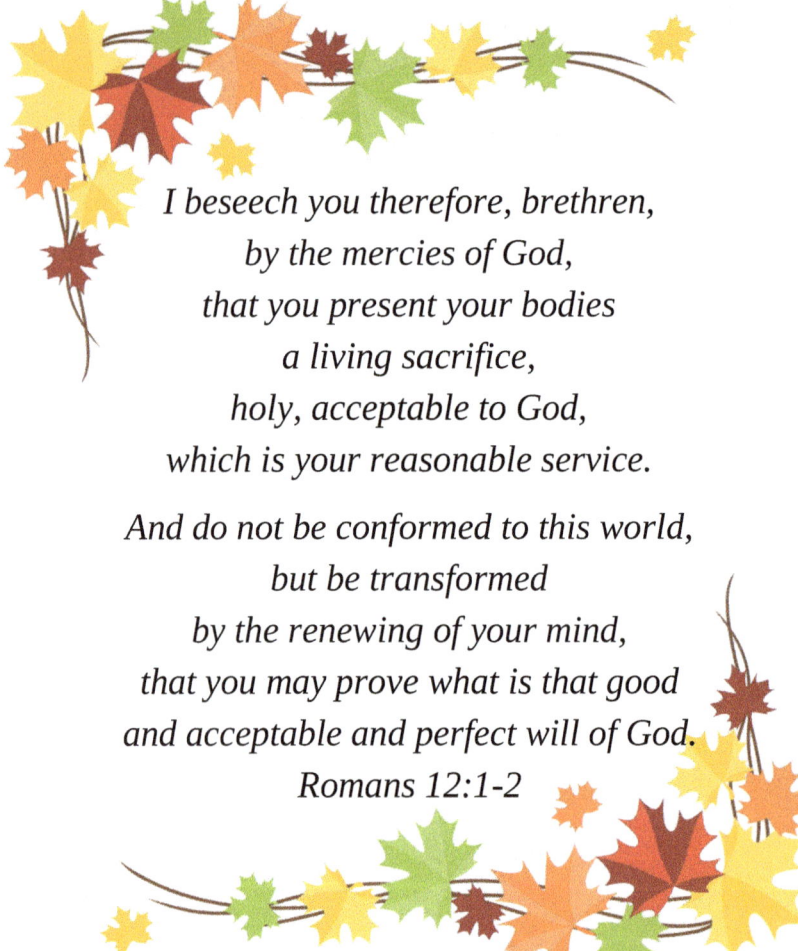

I beseech you therefore, brethren,
by the mercies of God,
that you present your bodies
a living sacrifice,
holy, acceptable to God,
which is your reasonable service.

And do not be conformed to this world,
but be transformed
by the renewing of your mind,
that you may prove what is that good
and acceptable and perfect will of God.
Romans 12:1-2

The Answer to My Journey

This Book

LET ME START THIS SECTION with one of the devotional blogs I have written:

Experiencing God: Neither a Template nor a Formula

While working on my book and studying the lives of men and women of faith in the Bible, I couldn't help but be amazed at how our loving God worked in the lives of each of them. Our Heavenly Father worked through them to manifest His power, love, and grace to mankind. Both the Old and New Testaments narrate their experiences for us to learn about and appreciate YHWH. The Holy Spirit then reminded me of the essence of these events.

Are these meant to be an example for us to follow? Should we expect a burning bush when God talks to us? Are we to be swallowed and spit out by a big fish when we purposely go in the other direction to what God told us? Are we to part the sea like Moses did? Are we to bring five loaves and two fish to the church potluck gathering to feed the entire congregation? Are we to bring a net and drop it on the 'other side' of the boat?

I truly believe that these miracles and wonders were done specifically for the people God was dealing with. Therefore, these chronicled events were not for the purpose of building a template for us to follow, or a formula to use repeatedly at our will. These are testimonies of God's character to encourage us to walk closely with Him every day.

We cannot and should not put God in a box, but we should enthusiastically expect God to keep His promises and meet us in **our** 'tent of meeting'.

> *"God made man because He loves stories."*
> (Elie Wiesel)

For these first seven scriptural personalities, were you able to relate to any of their stories, or maybe just an incident in their story? These narrations show us God's faithfulness, power and grace, and the Bible will use them to talk to us and guide us in a very personal way, and He will lead us to cross the sea of circumstances all around us.

Changing one's career sometimes creates a long transition process and might even be costly. But when the time has indeed come to change, He will definitely give you His assurance through His faithful promises and peace.

Faith in our Heavenly Father is of utmost importance in this relationship, as these people showed they had this faith, and when they (he) *"believed in the Lord, and He accounted it to him for righteousness."* The attitudes they showed in their journeys helped keep them on track on God's path for them. We must keep our time with the Lord sacred as communication is vital for both relationships and the change process. So, aim for that intimacy Moses had, for *"… the Lord spoke to Moses face to face, as a man speaks to his friend."* Exodus 33:11

If you are reading this book, you are then a witness to another great testimony of God's wonderful grace! He showed me at that point in my life I needed to change my career and that He would guide me through each intricate step of the way. And as an act of faith, I did!

> *"The Lord God is my strength;*
> *He will make my feet like deer's feet,*
> *And He will make me walk on my high hills."*
> Habakkuk 3:19

Additional Resource

A Deer Migration –

https://youtu.be/BIAyb-1uwTg

Tent of Meeting –

https://www.biblegateway.com/resources/dictionary-of-bible-themes/7474-Tent-Meeting

About the Author

Dion S. Tan works in corporate digital solutions in New Zealand as a change analyst, training analyst and business analyst. He is the founder and director of Kwinnovate Limited, New Zealand.

Dion is a disciple of Christ under the Navigators (Phils) Ministry, mentored to handle God's Words properly, building a growing relationship with Jesus and applying His truth in one's daily life. By the calling of God, Dion is now also a Christian author.

Dion was a member of a choral group as well as a church choir, and sang baritone or bass in a male quartet group. He was also a member of the children's ministry of various churches and worked as an EDGE facilitator, a mentorship program in schools for BB.ORG.NZ

ICONZ is a faith-based and church-based boys' outreach ministry of BB New Zealand, of which Dion is also a unit leader.

You can contact Dion at castyournetpublishing@gmail.com.
Dion can also be found on Facebook:
https://www.facebook.com/CastYourNetPublishing/

www.ingramcontent.com/pod-product-compliance
Lightning Source LLC
Chambersburg PA
CBHW062049290426
44109CB00027B/2777